Conscious Creation
Directing Energy to Get The Life You Want

Dee Wallace

OZARK
MOUNTAIN
PUBLISHING
PO Box 754, Huntsville, AR 72740
800-935-0045 or 479-738-2348 fax 479-738-2448
www.ozarkmt.com

For permission, serialization, condensation, adaptions, or for our catalog of other publications, write to Ozark Mountain Publishing, Inc., P.O. Box 754, Huntsville, AR 72740, ATTN: Permissions Department.

Library of Congress Cataloging-in-Publication Data
Wallace, Dee, 1948 -
    Conscious Creation - Directing Energy to Get the Life You Want;
Dee Wallace
How to create anything you want consciously by unleashing the power of your own energy!

1. Creating Reality   2. Energy   3. Metaphysics   4. Conscious Creation
I. Wallace, Dee, 1948-   II. Creating Reality   III. Title

Library of Congress Catalog Card Number: 2011928632

ISBN: 978-1-886940-26-0

Cover Art and Layout: www.noir33.com
Book set in: Times New Roman, Grand, Perpetua
Book Design: Julia Degan

Published by:

PO Box 754
Huntsville, AR 72740

WWW.OZARKMT.COM
Printed in the United States of America

Dedication

This book is dedicated to The One Consciousness of Us, and to the many teachers that enlightened my remembering of Who I Really Am: Dr. Soram Singh Khalsa, Dr. Sat-Kaur Khalsa, Jana Saunders, Dr. Cindy Larson, Dr. Daoshing Ni, Charles Conrad, Dr. Harry Morgan Moses and Debbie Luican.

I honor my many students that participated in the channeling of this information, in particular Nadia Angelini, Jennifer Connell and Jarrad Hewett. Most of all, I acknowledge my mother, Maxine Bowers, and my daughter, Gabrielle, who taught me unconditional love which is the key to all enlightenment.

Contents

You cannot understand from your mind.

You must experience with your heart.

That is knowing.

That is enlightenment.

That is love.

Introduction

IT IS TIME FOR US to be victors—not victims. To know—
not just hope.

We have been taught that the world happens and we react.
It is time for us to create the world we are reacting to.

All of this is possible. Indeed, it is the truth we must create
knowingly.

"Once in Kansas City, there was a little girl named Dee
Wallace, who dreamed of being a movie star. She took dancing
lessons, did her studies, worked hard. And when she grew up,
she went to Hollywood and became an actress. Then something
wonderful happened to her: She was cast in a movie with a
creature destined to be the summer's hottest star, E.T."

That was the cover page from an article in the Kansas City
Star immediately after E.T. opened. I had, by all standards,
"arrived." But the landing would be short lived. I had no idea
that the movie actually would be a metaphor for my own life
journey back—to me.

It is an ongoing journey, an ever-expanding and continuous
reevaluation and redirection into higher consciousness that
challenges me to choose being "home" in each moment of my
life. I have a lot to share with everyone about the passion of
healing.

This book was designed to give you a specific roadmap to
creating an abundant, happy, healthy life. It is not theory. It is
not conjecture. It is a book full of specific tools that can create
miraculous manifestations in your life. You simply must
decide you want to heal.

I am absolutely certain this material has been given to me
from the Highest Source. I know this beyond a doubt.

Information that I had absolutely no former knowledge of was channeled to me. At times, I had to study to understand what it meant!

The information here has changed my life, my family's lives, and the lives of my friends, students and co-workers. My very clear intention is that it changes yours.

Let me introduce some of my childhood patterns that became my perceptions of life. I was, for most of my life, the average Jane, raised in the Midwest in a very poor family. My mother worked full-time. My father worked when he could hold a job. He was an alcoholic, who ultimately committed suicide. I grew up believing and expecting that I couldn't depend on men, while seeing that the woman had to carry the load. Those were the lessons I was watching, which evolved into the beliefs I was ultimately committed to.

At the same time, I always felt incredibly loved by both my parents. But most of my childhood, from about age nine all the way through my high school years, was spent trying to rescue my mother from verbal and emotional abuse from my very drunken father, who usually was naked and berating her. This happened every night of my life that I can remember throughout my childhood years.

I saw my mother doing what she thought was her part, trying to be the defender, trying to take care of all of us. She believed she had to save everybody, which later became the role I chose in life. I was the little light in the family, the towheaded blonde, always happy and go lucky, but I dimmed my light because of the circumstances surrounding me. When you're young you forget you are your own creator. I believed this was the way the world was. Period.

Men, who represent to me not only fathers, but the people who keep us safe, the people who are supposed to support us, rarely showed up for me in my life. I was recreating what I knew. I attracted a lot of men into my life that I had to take care of in one way or another. I believed that if I didn't take care of everybody, everyone died. That's the message that I put together for myself when I was younger. So my energy was attracting men who would fulfill my belief—men I had to take care of. Because if they took care of me, *I* couldn't take care of everyone. And everyone died.

And then there was the success tape. I saw my father and mother try to start several different businesses. My father would get right to the point where he would almost be successful and then something would happen. Something would sabotage it or he would sabotage it. A building would burn to the ground. Someone would take his "invention" away from him. He would stop believing in himself. It was a pattern, one with which I'm sure many of you can identify: you almost get there and something sabotages the manifestation. In my 30s, I began to see the same pattern in my own life.

It is important to consciously identify all these patterns and belief systems that we have chosen to take on or to "own" from our childhood and elsewhere. We must know that we are the only ones who can energetically shift our perspectives in this lifetime and recreate those beliefs from a more balanced perspective. Otherwise we just pass them down all over again, even to ourselves in lives to come. My vote is to get it done in this lifetime and start creating the lives we want now. It's never too late.

One of the biggest misconceptions from my younger years is about my older brother, Denny, who was my hero. He was always my self-appointed "guardian." I thought he took care of us all. In my naiveté and youthfulness, that role had to belong to a "man." So I created it in my brother, even though it was my mother who was driving the ship and keeping us all afloat.

I remember my mother, my brother and me sitting in a "family meeting." I was too young to understand what was going on, maybe 7th grade. We were talking about Daddy and what to do about Daddy and how to solve the family problems. I think, quite frankly, I was in a fog and not really getting what it was all about. They started talking about money and middle class and the poor and Denny said, "Mom, right now we're about as poor as we're going to get." I remember taking this HUGE energetic hit in the gut, and I looked at him and said,

"Denny, we're not poor." He looked at me and said, "Oh, PeeWee, we're poor."

I can feel it now and it makes me want to cry. I was devastated by the fear that we were "poor." It created all kinds of panic in me. What's going to happen to me? How can we be poor? We have a house! Well, yes, we were renting a house, and my grandmother was paying for it, but I didn't know that. I know that the fear of being poor and the fear of not having enough has haunted me my entire life from that moment. Even though the Universe has always taken care of me, the reality is I've lived in the fear that I'm not taken care of, that the Universe won't take care of me. The illusion was my reality. That perception created a lot of my life.

I know from this work that it really doesn't have to do with what you have or where you are or what your reality "looks like." It has everything to do with what your "truth" is energetically. Until we know the higher truth, we keep creating from our limitations. I had to energetically shift the beliefs and the fears and the expectations of being "poor" that were creating my life. I had to become conscious that my "reality" wasn't real. It was only real because I believed it was real. I saw it that way, and I created it manifesting that way.

Even if I'm living in a mansion with servants, if my "reality" is that I'm still "poor" and I'm defining myself that way and I'm still holding those fears, I still live energetically in that "poorness." I limit myself in the creation of abundance because "poor" can't create more. If I am living in a mansion and still hold myself in lack consciousness, my energetic reality is fear of losing what I have or never experiencing my true abundance.

In either case, I keep myself from the truthfulness of the moment. The perception of lack defines me.

Not all perceptions limit us. Sometimes, we make empowering decisions in childhood. I was brought up Methodist, which is just about the easiest and most open of the Christian religions as far as dogma's concerned. I went to Bible school, and I was always taught to respect and love my church and my God. I remember often when, as a teenager, I would want to go out on Saturday night and stay out late, my mother would say, "If you can stay out late on Saturday night, you can get up for church on Sunday." And I always did.

At church, my mother directed all the religious dramas, the Easter pageant, and the Christmas play. We all performed in them. Daddy did the scenery, although he never attended church. Grandma made the costumes. Everyone was very active in the church. As a child who started out as baby Jesus and ended up as a young woman at the well, church and acting and family became one for me. I think those experiences forever connected my acting and my spirituality because I knew from a very early age that creativity came from a higher place. It had nothing to do with your head; it had everything to do with your heart. It wasn't by mistake that I ultimately ended up finding Charles Conrad, who taught that premise in acting: get out of your head and totally move into your instinctual heart. That connection from my childhood is one I don't want to reprogram. It was, and is, the truth. I spent many years trying to remember the truth of creating from my heart, but the constant fears that kept me from feeling "safe" kept me in my head and took me out of creation.

I immediately went into fear when my uncle came to get me at school in my senior year. One of the vice-principals pulled me out of class. I walked into the office, and I saw my uncle and I knew. I said, "Something's happened to Daddy, hasn't it?" As we walked out, he said, "Yes, something has happened to Daddy, and your mother's not here because she had to be medicated." That's what I remember anyway. I remember coming back to the house, and my mother was back on her bed. I thought she was asleep, but I'm sure she was sedated. My uncle proceeded to tell me that my father had committed suicide. He'd shot himself in the head. I don't think I really got any more information until my older brother came home. It's such a haze to me. I don't quite know how I got all the information. I remember saying that I wanted to tell my younger brother. That I would do it. He was only eight or nine at the time, but we were always close. I remember taking Damon upstairs and how hard it was.

We were living apart from my father at this point. My mother had finally decided that none of us could take it anymore. She had moved us all out months earlier. I know at some point, we all felt guilty about that. Thinking that if we'd stayed, it would have been different. I don't think it would have been different though. I know it wouldn't have. The reality, and the guilt I feel associated with that reality, are two entirely different things. My adult mind knows that now, but my child still formed the belief that if you leave, someone dies.

I keep going back to what happened and all the emotional and vibrational limiting beliefs that I created. In essence, the things that create our lives are the choices and vibrations we create in response to what happens. These vibrations set up repetitive frequencies that we keep generating and holding on to. They create more fear. As long as we perceive the world as a place to fear, we attract fear into our lives. It is our expectation. If I hold onto the notion that men never show up for me, they won't. I create that. Those are the men I vibrate with. If I expect that I'm abandoned by the person who's supposed to take care of me, then that's the vibration the Universe resonates with and responds to.

It's almost like the match game. OK, you're creating this energy, I'll come forward to match that. That's why so many of us are not creating the lives we want because we are saying, "I don't want what I've created," and yet we're not taking any steps to create something else. The Universe responds with, "I can match that. I will show up for you exactly as you believe."

The Universe is doing its part. We're just confused around our part, our role in this relationship. We are not saying what we WANT.

There always comes the conundrum of which comes first, the chicken or the egg. How can I possibly feel better when I don't have enough money to pay my rent, I've just found out I have cancer, or my significant other has just left me or beaten me? How do you start feeling good about that, Dee? I'm saying to you, there are ways. There are definite steps that you can take to start moving your vibration and frequencies to a higher level, if you choose to consciously shift. It's not an overnight explosion, but the steady purposeful process of enlightenment. I guarantee you that when you do this, the Universe will start showing up in different ways for you. It all starts with you.

We absolutely must move out of our victim consciousness. Whatever was "done" to us when we were little, whatever our stories are, whatever the beliefs and the fears that have affected us, we must redirect, reprogram and nurture now. We must create new perceptions of ourselves and the world based on our new perspectives. That's impossible to do if we stay in the victim consciousness of the past.

Think of your life as a radio station. Say you want to tune into happiness, and happiness is only at 107.5 on your radio dial, and you keep tuning in to 105, which is depression, or 102.3, which is anger or judgment. You're never going to hit the right frequency to get the "happy" station. That's what most of us are doing. We are tuning in to what we don't want. We have to consciously choose to tune into the higher vibration, so that we can attract and create the things we want.

For years after my daughter was born, I was on the health circuit, in the healing circles, the positive thinking space, the affirmation place. Still, I wasn't creating the life I wanted. Nobody I knew was creating the life they wanted. And I wanted to know why. I asked God, Buddha, Mohammed, Universal love, whatever term you relate to as the highest Source. I was asking the Creative Force to give me understanding and guidance. Answers started flooding in.

Many of us are in the middle of this journey. We've made some steps forward, but not enough to reap what it is we want. Once I began consciously creating, I started to turn my life around. So will you.

The catalyst for this change was a little movie called E.T. As soon as I did E.T., for a number of reasons, many of my dormant fears took over. My "knowing" fell out. I fell out of being my own creator. I plunged into the false belief that creation belongs to others, to fate, and to "circumstances beyond our control." I became really angry, really judgmental, and a victim all over again.

The Creative Force works in mysterious ways. I believe that I had to go through this experience in order to learn everything that I had to learn, in order to write this book, in order to get this information and get it out to the world. I've discovered the truth and the knowing.

It's also interesting that my acting technique, which I've used for over thirty years, mirrors what I've learned over these last eight years: it's all based in energy, go to your heart, allow your natural instinct to guide you, come from love, and let yourself be a channel. You are always in the moment.

Even back when I was starting my career, the Universe was leading me to the truth. It's all about energy. It's all about how you vibrate. It's not about what you say or even about the thoughts that you think, but it is about the energy that's creating why you say or think those thoughts. As the actor James Dean said, "It's not about the words." I am indebted to Charles Conrad for teaching these principles in acting that truly mirror life.

Different people manifest things in completely different ways. Some people are exceptionally successful in their businesses and can't create success in relationships at all. Some people are horrible in business and can't make any money, but are loving and nurturing in their relationships. Some people are brilliant in business and end up creating illness as a side note in their lives. These all have to do with energy and the frequencies we're vibrating at, created largely from perceptions we hold.

Most of us know on some level that we've lost our way. We were, in the beginning, greater beings than what we have become. We know in our hearts that we want to get back to the beings we were born to be. It's absolutely possible to do that. There will be ideas contained in this book that you have probably heard of before but will hear from a new perspective. There will also be new ideas and practices in this book that will give you actual tools, beyond affirmations, beyond hope, beyond visualization to create what you want.

The Universe served it up perfectly to create this work through my acting studio, a business I thought I started for financial remuneration. I now believe the acting studio was created to develop this work. When the healing information started coming in, truthfully, none of us knew what was going on. We didn't know what we were dealing with. It is because I had such endearing love with my students, and trust from them, that they plunged into this exploration of the truth. They went into trust about this work and decided they were going to be a part of it. I honor every single one of my students for whatever section of this work they helped to create.

All these students were ready, willing, and able to incorporate this work with the acting and go into a much deeper place. We were using it to delve into deep, personal blocks that were affecting their performances. It became apparent that many of us shared most of these blocks, and, ultimately, so did our families and friends. We soon had a sense that we were doing work, not just for ourselves, but for the world. That became our intention: to heal ourselves on behalf of all Energy. If I hadn't had that pool of people around me, I don't know how I would have been able to create this work. If I'd been a scientist, I'd have had to fund a study. The Universe funded the study for me.

Like me, whoever you are and whatever you're doing in this moment is a perfect place to start this work. Indeed, it is the only place. It is the work itself. Many of us are trying to use our daily jobs as our definitions of self. But the journey—the process—is the coming home if we choose that perspective in each moment. However, and whatever, we use to get home is the work of this lifetime: how we choose to create each moment is our ultimate defining cause.

The Journey Begins

Chapter 1

The Creation of My Life Journey

IT IS BY NO ACCIDENT that I ended up as Mary, the mom in E.T. The picture perfectly mirrors my own life journey, and probably yours as well. E.T. was trying to get home—back to his roots, back to his family, back to where his heartlight got recharged. Back to love.

He had been left behind, abandoned, was scared, confused, and didn't know what to do. Until he took action to override his fears, it looked pretty grim. But he never gave up his belief he would get home, and with that belief, he manifested his dream into reality. It definitely was a journey he chose to create.

We all feel on some level abandoned, scared and confused—not knowing what to do to get home to the happiness we really are. The movie is a metaphor for the life journey. In retrospect, it's almost as if the Universe was prepping me with a mini life lesson for the multitude of lessons to come. Had I been truly conscious, I probably could have learned the lessons in two months, rather than the two decades it took to achieve. And I'm still learning because creation is ongoing.

Soul lessons are always ongoing. We are continually in the process of expanding. We are on an accelerated consciousness shift in this world. We are being asked to come forward and remember the power of the Creative Force. It's who we are. We are being encouraged to claim that, activate it, and thereby define a consciousness of creation rather than a reactionary victim consciousness that's still based in limited perceptions and beliefs. Humankind has always been called to raise itself up to greater self-awareness. The consciousness of the planet, indeed, the creation of our future, is mandating a quantum shift in accepting and actuating Self-Creation. We must come forward, positively creating our own lives, and raise the vibration of the planet. If you are reading this, you are part of it. This work facilitates quantum leap movement forward into higher awareness and consciousness. It leads you "home."

E.T. gave it to us simply:

1. Know what you want.
2. Release the blocks and fears in the way (i.e. change your perceptions.)
3. Take action.
4. BELIEVE
5. Most importantly, keep your heart light on! If your heartlight goes out, you are in darkness.

My heart center was closed for about twenty years. At least it wasn't open consistently. I'm sure it opened up at the conception and birth of my daughter and various other highpoints, but I was holding so much anger that it wasn't open much.

I absolutely had a right to be angry. I had been given more than my share of hardships in my first thirty years—a debilitating childhood, father abandonment, poverty. I felt I had been sabotaged by someone to the point where my career was over. It was unjust. It broke my heart. My heart light went completely off to protect myself "from more harm." At the time, I didn't know that I created it all. Yep. If I walk my talk about what I am teaching you here, I have to know I attract my life to me because of the beliefs and energetic vibrations I hold in my energy field. Unconsciously, of course. But, nevertheless, my own. If you point the finger at someone else, you better turn it around! See, even E.T.'s finger comes back into play!

I digress. I was hurt and in pain. I was in fear because not only was my dream ripped away, but my livelihood as well. Pain and fear: the conditions that create fertile ground for anger. Look at our world. School shootings, road rage, high divorce rates. Anger is everywhere. We are feeling scared and alone. I was totally abandoned—much like E.T.—by agents, friends, and co-workers, who just didn't want to "make waves," all a representation of my own energy, how I was feeling about myself. I felt scared and alone, but I had to stop pointing the finger at the rest of the world to see the gift in my own healing.

I began to understand how I had woven my own sticky web. First, I realized it was my fears and my expectations that drew these experiences into my life, so I could consciously see my negative patterns and choose not to create them anymore. I had to choose to see the world differently: the way I wanted it to be. Once I was ready to move out of my own lower vibration, I attracted people and circumstances to MATCH my HIGHER VIBRATIONS and the world seemed to "all of a sudden" love me. I began to see the world in a new way. Because I was learning to love myself, I began to reclaim my own life creation. Like E.T., I started compiling the components to get back home. "What you see is what you get" is not just an antiquated statement your grandmother used. It represents a scientific fact: focus = manifestation.

E.T. created love and friendship in a world where he didn't fit in. The Universe rushed to support his journey. I'm not pointing fingers at anyone but myself. When I learned to do that while loving myself, my healing took a big leap. It's a vital step in moving forward. The proverbial buck stops with us.

It was—and still is—a process. I struggled against myself to be who I really was. I was pure light in my original and natural being, but the more I focused on the injustice and betrayal, the more my light dimmed. My vibrations

5

plummeted, and work fell away. My health began to fail. Back problems, high blood pressure, and headaches, none of which I had ever been prone to before, became everyday occurrences. I even contracted Epstein Barr, or Chronic Fatigue Syndrome. No wonder. I was battling the biggest soul lesson I had to learn: I create my own life. If I wanted to get me back, it was up to me. That's a little hard to do when you're a victim that is being "held down" and it's "everyone else's fault!"

One day, I fell to my knees in tears and told whoever was listening, "I CAN'T DO THIS ANYMORE. I don't want to be this way anymore. I want to get back to me." That, simply, is how the work began. I knew I was a person who wanted to heal, a person who wanted her light back. And I knew I wanted us all to heal ourselves. Like E.T., I was ready to go home.

Slowly, I was led to different healers who educated me and helped me through my own journey by teaching me about energy and how to move and focus it in order to create. I learned how to run energy through my hands to shrink a large fibroid tumor that was preventing me from becoming pregnant. I had already learned an acting technique based on energy. I learned about taking my own healing back. It was my own responsibility. I had to be energetically involved with healing myself. This was the biggest catalyst in moving my life forward because I consciously chose to be responsible for myself.

I am in agreement that doctors and healers serve a valuable purpose. They allow us to give our fears and trust "to someone who knows," which releases our energy flow, releases resistance to believing we can heal, and moves us into "letting go" so healing can take place. But ultimately, we heal ourselves. Energetically, we allow lower, negative vibrations, beliefs, and fears to be balanced so we can be at choice. When we balance those frequencies that attracted illness and unhappiness into our consciousness, we send out new, higher vibrations that begin attracting more health and happiness into our lives. We don't vibrate and attract dis-ease. We vibrate and attract health. We vibrate and attract healing relationships and abundance. Most of all, we attract loving ourselves. When I truly learned, again, that I am responsible for creating my life because I am the Creative Force, I began to heal more consistently. I could "hold" the higher vibrations easier and for longer periods of time. As challenges appeared to resurface, my negative reaction time decreased exponentially. I began living in peace and consciousness. By choice. New challenges still appear, and I still have negative reactions. It is the ongoing process of always choosing to feel good.

I was able to acknowledge how important perceptions are to all the ways you affect and use (or don't use) energy to create what you want to manifest. I learned it goes way beyond thought. I learned how energies from past generations, past lives, wronged relationships, and misguided perceptions can literally poison our energy field. Every bit of information in this book was born from an experience that strengthened me. That makes all of it "good."

Some of this information, as it was being made known to me, was at times beyond what my mind could comprehend. Like E.T., I was in a foreign land, alone. Often, I was forced to simply keep an open mind while the clarity and truthfulness was made apparent to me. Keep in mind I am just a simple girl from Kansas who had your fairly basic Methodist upbringing. Many of these concepts forced me to expand my comfort zone beyond what I thought was possible. Keep an open mind and "feel" your own truth. Some things may be instant. Others may never be comfortable for you. I was challenged by all those reactions while the work was developing. Once it was complete, I knew unconditionally the truthfulness of this work from my life's dramatic re-creation. As they say, once you cross the mountain, it's a whole new view. Keep your heartlight on.

Chapter 2

Perfection of the Creative Force

IT IS HUMBLING WHEN I look back and recognize the perfection of the Creative Force in leading me to open an acting studio to develop this work. I could have just as easily done it teaching high school English, which I've done, or waiting tables, or being a CPA (although I'm dreadful in math!) You can find the highest truth right where you are. For me, it was teaching acting. It's all about asking for answers, and you can do that now, this moment, in whatever you do and wherever you are.

After my career began to enter a slower period, I had to look for other ways to make a living. I needed consistent money because I believed I didn't have enough because I had been victimized. See the beliefs? I have a high school teaching credential; I'm an excellent communicator and love to teach. Teaching seemed to be the most logical option. Teaching acting was the obvious choice—I could set my own hours, as opposed to public school, and I had a following. So in 1995, I opened up the Dee Wallace Stone Acting Studio. I had five attendees. By the end of the first year, I had a full class. For the next eleven years I had between 65 and 80 students on an ongoing basis.

As my mentor Charles Conrad before me, I teach from the basis of energy. The technique is all based on energy. Another way the Universe was schooling me for the bigger picture and the healing work. Basically, the technique works like this: get your energy extremely high so that it bypasses the conscious

9

mind. When you get out of your mind, you move into your intuition, and creativity just takes over.

We all have experiences of this in our lives. Usually, we're forced into them. Pulling someone from a burning car requires immediate instinct. Pushing yourself to do something you're afraid to do, like hang gliding, requires you to move into instinct. You jump past the logical parameters of your conscious mind and just act. You are in play with the Universe. The next steps are: know what you want to achieve in the scene, and then DON'T DECIDE HOW YOU ARE GOING TO PLAY IT. Allow the higher energy to channel through you to create your manifestation of the character in the most unique, creative way possible. Basically, it takes you into your heart and out of your logic, into the truthfulness of Source and out of control. That is the basis of any creative life: living in the heart and not the mind.

That's exactly how the Creative Force works. We have to

1. Know what we want
2. Move into creative intuition
3. Direct the Creative Force to create it in its most fabulous of ways (not our picture of how it is to look!)
4. Know it will be manifested

These are all integral parts of manifestation. They keep us in the effortless flow of not having to control the particulars of how something is manifested and allowing it to manifest in its highest form. If you are worried, fearful, resentful, doubtful, or unsure, your mind says, "Take charge. Control!" Any actor who is terrified he'll mess up can't create. The energy gets stuck. Life is the same. The joy is choosing to flow and trust. The joy is in the doing and in living the moments. The joy is the process. Life, after all, is the greatest part we'll ever play.

As I look back on those years with gifted, talented, hungry, spiritual people, I see that the Universe was indeed giving me what I asked for: a way for all people to heal themselves. It manifested in a way I could never have imagined. For the last six years of the studio, I had a consistent group of actors—souls called to be lightworkers on the planet—helping develop this healing work, testing the work, trying the work, refining it, and witnessing the results.

I asked for a way people, who had no psychic, no metaphysical teacher, priest, or psychiatrist to help them, could heal themselves. A way to reach the masses. Source created an acting studio to bring it about. It had also schooled me in many of the concepts I would be asked to use and explore.

Quickly, I'm going to give you a rundown of how this work was created. I began working first with spiritual psychologist Dr. Sat-Kaur Khalsa and physician Dr. Soram Singh Khalsa, both of whom used and introduced me to the art of kinesiology, or muscle testing. Kinesiology is the art of connecting to the Higher Energy to get clear, concise answers removed from the lower plane consciousness of ego. It is done through testing the strength and resistance of muscles. If a statement is truthful energetically, it strengthens you and also your muscles. If it is not, it weakens you. Organs, food, thoughts and beliefs, which are all energy, can be tested with this method. It is a powerful way to discern subconscious energy that may be weakening you. I began practicing this on my own with the intention of always receiving the highest answer. The use of kinesiology was limited, however because I needed someone to help me by testing the strength of my arm. (There are other methods of self-kinesiology, such as using your fingers.)

I began using kinesiology to teach extended lessons on energy within the acting studio. I read everything to educate myself. It became apparent that many of the students—and I—needed to learn a different way of testing so we could do the work by ourselves. After all, that was what I initially asked for—a way people could heal themselves, by themselves. Using a pendulum was my next step in self-reliance. A pendulum is usually a gemstone of some kind suspended by a

11

chain or string. The chain is held between the thumb, index finger, and middle finger while the stone dangles. Actually, you can even use a necklace or a tea bag! Each person has a distinct swing pattern for "yes," which mirrors the strength of the arm in kinesiology, and a "no," which represents weak muscles. Therefore, by using yes/no statements, this allows a person to test energy on their own.

Around that time I was led to a NAET practitioner named Cindy Larson. NAET, or Nambudripad's Allergy Elimination Techniques was developed by an Indian woman named Devi S. Nambudripad, M.D. I went to Cindy to work on eliminating allergies and toxins. Source had a much greater plan. Cindy used a pendulum to test much of her work. I watched with awe the discernment and accuracy she was able to achieve with this tool. I began practicing.

At this time, I was also becoming consistently aware that when I needed something, it began showing up. It was more than just luck. I realized I was truly affecting my own life. This realization was so overwhelming I actually became a little frightened. To think you are in charge of your own life was a new and daunting idea. I wasn't quite sure how I was doing it, but I could see the synchronicity in my life. I knew I was working with energy, but I was still not clear that I was directing energy or how I was directing energy.

Again, I was ready for my next life course: Consciously Directing Energy 101. While I was working with Cindy Larson and Drs. Khalsa, I was in my early 30's and I wanted to get pregnant. Seven specialists told me I never would. But I knew. I wanted that baby so much my entire focus was on creating her, and the Universe responded. I was led to an acupuncturist, Dr. Dao Shing Ni, who was instrumental in helping me get pregnant. He taught me how to run energy through my hands: to literally DIRECT the energy physically to shrink a fibroid tumor.

This was a huge realization and a major component of the work: I actually could direct physical energy. I still wasn't aware of the need to direct all energy on a day-to-day conscious level, but the success I had in using my hands to shrink my tumor and create physical results was proof of the ability and validity that energy could be directed by me! It was my introduction to energy transmutation.

After six years of trying to conceive, I produced a beautiful baby girl that seven "specialists" said I would never have. I had said I wanted that baby and I created her! Even with this success, the healing work was in its infant stage. I still didn't realize exactly how I created that baby—that I was creating what was happening in my life. I was still creating unconsciously. I wasn't "conscious" that I was transmuting energy. I knew I had participated, but was not quite sure how. I couldn't believe it. It was so foreign from everything I had ever been taught.

I decided to begin asking the Universe—the higher knowledge—to guide me to clarity by using the pendulum. After releasing my fear that I was manipulating the energy and that my information was not coming from the Highest Source, the pendulum became an invaluable tool to access higher information. Think of it merely as a telephone to receive information you need from the Creative Force. I began teaching that tool. I used the pendulum initially to find which beliefs and fears were blocking me. We became proficient at discerning what the blocks were. Cindy Larson introduced my first experience in tangibly transmuting energy.

She taught me the process by which you tapped out a negative belief and circled in a positive one. This process replaced the belief of the negative and implanted the positive belief. At least that was our understanding at the time. It was tedious and time-consuming, but it was the beginning of the most exciting learning curve I've ever experienced. Two years into the work, we were given the discernment that we were really BALANCING all energy. Like nature, our intention was to create and maintain a balance in all energy. Again, I had so many students willing to help with these basic levels, the time element was decreased exponentially.

Ultimately, we reached the point of understanding that we simply had to transmute energy by our intention and direction. Let me restate that: through our intention and direction. We knew we were on the right track because the more we balanced, the more our lives started opening up. Each time we used the work to balance, another limitation was addressed and released. The energy was raised to the next highest level. A perfect process of refinement has been revealed as we have been guided through the journey.

As I look back, I can see the trail of breadcrumbs the Creative Force so perfectly laid out. As soon as I was ready, that trail was revealed to lead me where I needed to be next. Subject to subject, teacher to teacher. I can look back and see the Universe was working for all good. I had to learn to trust that. I'm still learning to trust that!

What all these practitioners had in common was that they used and directed energy to receive information and heal. That is how they heal, and that is how people heal themselves. When your life changes because of your direction, you can't deny the truth of the manifestations. Because of our growing experiences, we were, in fact, transmuting energy in our lives. Babies were being conceived, careers were taking off, relationships were being enhanced or created, and health was improving. Things were being created by our conscious application of this work. We weren't merely believers. We knew it worked.

Transmuting energy is easier than you think. You have to start with wanting to change your energy. Then you must choose to believe you can. My students and I did. Because of those beliefs, we moved into that knowing, and because we requested answers, the Creative Force started giving them. We began to realize that as we transmuted energy, it affected everything: our physical as well as our emotional and psychological health. Changing the vibrations affected EVERY ASPECT OF OUR LIVES.

At one point, I realized the breadcrumbs led me back to me. I was no longer looking outside of myself. I was the source of the information I was seeking because I was a part of the One Energy that is everything. I began "hearing" answers. This is known as clairaudience. We are all naturally born to be instinctive in all ways. It is our self-limitation that keeps us from hearing, from knowing. So, during all this time, I began hearing guidance, oftentimes while I was looking for answers for students. That is the best way I can describe the process when new information is given, a sort of knowingness that you heard the information. Think of the V8(R) advertisements. The actor would slap his forehead and remember that he should have had a V8(R). That's much like how it felt when information would drop in. Only because we had a way to test the validity—with many people receiving positive acknowledgment—did we learn to unconditionally trust what we were "hearing." Then, of course, the class and I would test the correctness of the information. The information began with the more basic elemental fears and limiting beliefs of this plane: health, abundance, relationships. It then grew to include genetic ties, then moved to the higher and more spiritual energetic blocks that needed to be removed so higher consciousness could be obtained. For four years we painstakingly recorded and refined the information. We didn't understand until much later that whenever we balanced for one person, we were balancing for the whole, the Collective Consciousness, and all energy. It was our beginning realization that nothing is separate. All is One, consisting of differently defined energy pockets.

Different types of energy that affect our total energy field began coming into our consciousness. One type felt literally like outside forces or entities. We joked about being the overly dramatic creatures that actors can tend to be! We now understand that the energy is really our own fears, which would be ignited, grow and take us over. We would feel overwhelmed and out of control, which attracted similar vibrations to respond to us. Think of a group riot: it can start very small and soon be consumed by the larger response. Back then, we actually understood this energy as ghost-like energy. It is interesting that we were introduced to this energy in the easiest way we could understand it at our level. We've all seen the movies. We know how ghosts can take us over! That was how Source communicated the concept to us originally. Our understanding at that time was that an entity was an unhealed, stuck energy that attaches to our energy during vulnerable moments in our lives. Those energies were trying to heal and merge with the light again. "They" can negatively affect us because of the vibrations they pull us into. Our religions and the beloved movie world have created these energies as malevolent ghosts. I love the line in *The Sixth Sense*: "Did you ask them what they want?" Once the energy was helped, it "left." That was our experience. Once the energy was balanced, it could detach and move to the light. Once we controlled our fears, we moved back into creation.

I'll never forget when an "entity" first made an "appearance" in my Tuesday night class. If we hadn't already raised our energy to know that it was all good, we could have gone into a melodramatic panic. We literally identified and felt energies that had attached to our energy field (the sum of our physical, mental, emotional, chemical, cosmic and dimensional energy.) At first introduction this felt like huge resistance, or blocked energy. We experienced it as someone trying to tell us something but we couldn't hear them. Actually, it was our higher selves yelling, "Heal this!" We could only experience "their" presence. Because of our limited understanding, our first experiences with entities were a little frightening, simply because of our earthly beliefs and superstitions, our perceptions. When we finally ascertained, through the use of muscle testing, that "they" were indeed asking for help to leave our energy systems and get back to the light, their presence became an accepted and factual part of the work of transmuting lower vibrations to higher ones. They were coming forward to be balanced of negativity and be lifted out of our energy system, so they were not affecting us vibrationally. "They" could return to the light.

This was done by using kinesiology to direct us to the belief on the channeled information sheets that we had compiled that needed to be transmuted. Compare it to a child who wants to swim but had a negative experience with the water. Someone must transmute, or change and replace, that experience with a positive one, creating new and positive vibrations around water and swimming. Then the child can move into her power, let go of holding on, and begin to swim! It is the same concept for any type of energy. The vibrations need to be raised and the energy balanced so it can move and attract like energy that is higher vibration, creating our desires. We realized that "ghosts" are our fears within us, resisting healing because they are protecting us.

The healing work in this book facilitates this process for us. It is an exciting shift in channeling higher information and knowledge. It allows us to become the unemotional observer of our world. We know this is happening because synchronicities, information, and guidance begin presenting themselves in unmistakable ways to direct us. Three people recommend the same book, or a song comes on directly relating to your challenges. The Creative Force is in constant communication with us. Most of us just don't know the language.

In the beginning, it would sometimes take us a half hour just to get a piece of information. Because we were laden with so many levels of fears, false expectations, and judgments, it was laborious to receive the higher truths. We were asking ourselves to reevaluate our entire understanding about how creation works. It can be easier for you.

The good news: Source has cleared the path. Because of thousands of lightworkers in the world, the Collective Consciousness has been raised to such an extent that moving into higher consciousness is easier and quicker. However, each individual still has to choose to walk the path into higher consciousness. Lightworkers everywhere have helped quicken the journey, but each soul must consciously choose to start walking. We simply opened up the energy to allow the desire for healing to manifest, which means we can begin to create our lives in a more conscious way sooner. The Hundredth Monkey Phenomenon illustrates this perfectly.

In 1952, on an island in Japan, scientists were giving sweet potatoes dropped in the sand to the island monkeys. Even though they disliked the dirt on the sweet potatoes, the monkeys ate the dirty potatoes anyway, until a young monkey found that she could improve the taste by washing them in the water. She showed her mother and her friends and they all began to wash their sweet potatoes.

The young monkeys all began washing the sweet potatoes and showing their parents, who imitated their young. However, the other adults continued to eat the dirty sweet potatoes. Until one day, the "hundredth monkey" learned to wash the sweet potato! At that point all the monkeys started washing their sweet potatoes and, surprisingly, monkeys on *other* islands miles away spontaneously started washing their potatoes. The consciousness of potato washing had jumped across water! When the Collective Consciousness shares a vibration, information is shared automatically.

"When a certain critical number achieves an awareness, this new awareness may be communicated from mind to mind. Although the exact number may vary, this Hundredth Monkey Phenomenon means that when only a limited number of people know of a new way, it may remain the conscious property of these people. But there is a point at which if one more person tunes in to a new awareness, a field is strengthened so that this awareness is picked up by almost everyone." (The Hundredth Monkey by Ken Keyes Jr.)

This doesn't mean that all will be healed. Some of us will choose not to heal. We choose to come to this plane because our souls grow from the experiences of the physical world of disease, hate, judgment, and loss. Some of us will choose to stay in those lower vibrations and experiences instead of transmuting the energy to a higher vibration. This work does allow us to access our lessons that we have set out to learn at a faster pace if we so choose, thus enabling us more peaceful, positive experiences during the present incarnation. That contributes to the healing of the Collective Consciousness. All are One. No man is an island. When the majority of mankind learns, we all learn, and vice versa.

Like the monkeys, the work we did individually branched out into the energy of our mates, families, and eventually creation, incorporating all. This was confusing at first because when we were transmuting energy for ourselves, we would get stopped. We realized through our yes/no dialogue, accessed through kinesiology, that we were being directed to transmute energy for someone OTHER THAN OURSELVES. Even though we knew everyone creates for themselves, we did understand that through our intention to balance the energy within ourselves, we were somehow affecting The Energy, which allowed ALL energy to shift if it so chose.

First it began for family members, then friends, and it kept extending out. The pattern became continually clearer. The more energy we balanced, the more energy became incorporated. The work was extending out exponentially. The more light you add to a dark room, the less dark you have in the room, until eventually the light envelopes the entire dark. That's what was happening with the work. Soon we were being directed to raise vibrations for countries and, eventually, all of creation in the continuing education that energy is all encompassing. All energy is striving to be balanced. Each piece of energy you transmute and raise within yourself is transmuted for all creation. You really do affect your world.

It is important to note that we never do any work without getting permission from the Creative Force or a person's Higher Self. That is built into the work. If a person's soul does not want to participate, this work will not interfere. The intention is not to change someone, only to heal ourselves. We are only serving the One Energy on behalf of the whole. Heal yourself, heal the world.

According to our information, once a particular vibration, such as fear, has been balanced, that particular frequency doesn't have to be revisited on that level. The process then takes us to the next higher, more challenging levels of the similar blocks. Balancing energy to connect and live in higher consciousness is a process. Like any journey, one has to proceed at the pace his energy is comfortable with. We know from exhaustively testing the information that we were directed to do work on behalf of the world and creation, and that this work continues to expand. The exciting news is that each person's involvement expands it exponentially.

What I love about the work the Creative Force has provided us with is that it is simple, straightforward, and you don't have to revel around dramatically purging your guts, which often times feeds the very negativity you're looking to release. Source asks that you simply acquaint yourself with all information, so when you use the work, it is subconsciously AUTOMATICALLY INCORPORATED into your healing process. Right now, our task is to transmute our own fears, limitations and judgments to a high vibration, so we all contribute to the 100th Monkey. We choose to heal ourselves because we choose to heal the world. We choose to live in love.

Like E.T., we have to learn a new language and stop being scared and blaming those who abandoned and frightened us. We must become our own creator, take action, and allow our dreams to be manifested. It is my honor and blessing to share this very powerful work with you. Welcome to the journey of a lifetime!

There is specific groundwork that needs to be in place for this work to create in its greatest form. Like any journey back home, when you are lost, it helps to follow the breadcrumbs you've dropped along your way to get back, and you have dropped many. You just aren't conscious of what they are. This work creates a clear direction to finding that trail so you can heal and find your way home again to that happy, higher vibrational, loving place where you are powerful and safe and whole: where you are the creator once again.

The next few chapters explain the groundwork specifically. It is important for you to read them so your subconscious has all the information. The simple knowledge and acknowledgement of these principles creates important energy shifts.

Basically, the truths we need to embrace that enhance conscious creation are as follows:

1. Everything is energy. Energy is changeable. It vibrates on lower and higher frequencies. The same energy exists on several different planes and dimensions at the same time because we exist as holograms. All are One Energy, one Creative Force. That energy needs direction from you, who chooses how to direct it.

2. The intention you hold when you create anything is taken into the creation itself. If your intention is selfish, fearful, or of a lower vibration, that vibration is taken into the creation. It is your first direction.

3. You are in partnership with the Creative Force. Because you must direct the energy with your Choice, you actually are in charge of creating your own experiences out of the energy you direct.

4. You make a choice to live in lower or higher vibrations. Lower vibrations create more reactionary choices: retaliation, judgment, and self-abuse. Higher vibrations move us into choice of creation instead of reaction: understanding, acceptance, and self-love. It is really about consciously choosing to remain balanced, so you are at choice.

5. Since all is One Energy, you must know that you ARE the One Energy. This gives you permission and authority to create.
6. Forgiveness. If you don't move on from holding others responsible, you stay a victim. Victims don't create the lives they want. Believe it or not, you can live in total forgiveness because it's your choice. It is possible. Remember, you are forgiving them so you will live the life you desire.
7. Strive for gratitude.
8. Play. Have fun. Be as a little child. That is Creation.

If you retrace and rebalance your energetic breadcrumbs, it will take you back to the Creator you truly are. This is the groundwork that enables quantum leap movement in our work! These are the initial eight basic foundation pillars that create your life.

Chapter 3

Focused Energy

EVERYTHING IS ENERGY. MOST OF us learned this in fifth grade science. Energy can be manipulated, moved, and altered, but it's still energy, whether it's solid, liquid, or gas. Ice melts into water, water can be heated into steam, and steam can be condensed back into water.

Our bodies are no exception. They are also made up of energy. So are our thoughts and emotions. Everything is energy. This energy vibrates in frequencies. We are, essentially, walking vibrations. Like radio station, the frequency we vibrate at is what we broadcast out to the world around us. It also determines what we tune in to.

Most people know that emotions affect our physical bodies, our vibrational frequencies. People with high blood pressure are told to eliminate stress in their lives because stress can contribute to their high blood pressure. What is stress? The dictionary defines stress as the "internal resistance to applied force." In spiritual work, this translates into "being in resistance to Source and applying force upon self to control for safety." In other words, we are believing society's messages about what we have to do to survive, instead of flowing with Source. If I am vibrating with fear, stress, or lack of trust, my energy is being focused in a lower vibrational way, resisting flow. Because we need to define things, we call this "negative energy." It's an emotional, physical, mental or chemical response that causes disease in our energy. It is energy being focused in a particular way. There are three basic ways that affect how energy is focused during a lifetime:

1. Everything that has happened to us from our conception adds to how we define and shape our energy.
2. Genetic predispositions help define and shape our energy.
3. The vibrations we create, manifest, and bring into this life add to the total mix.

Number one is self-explanatory.

In number two, we know that genetic energy created our hair color, eye color, and physical build, but even our personalities are composed of some genetic energy. How many times have you heard, "He's just like his father?" That's because along with the hair color, your parents passed down beliefs and thoughts in the form of energy that is a part of your DNA. It keeps your cells genetically vibrating with certain expectant energy. Remember, everything is energy. Your DNA is energy. Your DNA includes all energy you were created with, joining your parents' DNA into yours and your grandparents', and so on. Their energetic predispositions are as much a part of you as your blue eyes. I believe this is the true meaning of "sins of the fathers." The limiting, fearful, lower vibrations have literally been passed down from generation to generation.

Then there is the third set of vibrations—those of our own that we bring in from many previous lifetimes that are still affecting our field of consciousness. These beliefs, fears, and judgments were formed by us in other incarnations and brought into this existence. Why are some of us born with unexplained illnesses, fears, musical tendencies, foreign language dispositions, or unusual physical abilities? The attributes that don't have their roots in this lifetime experience and make no sense genetically in the family predispositions must be active in our field of consciousness when we already are emerging into a new re-creation of embodiment.

The sum total of our life, past lives, and our genetic predispositions help to create the frequencies we vibrate with in this lifetime. It is that vibration, which feeds our perceptions of the world and ourselves, that resonates with energy to create manifestation. Just like a radio station attracts certain types of listeners, our vibrations attract like vibrations.

Our vibrations can mutate in confusing ways. For example, if your parents were bigots and transferred that energy into your DNA, it might look the same (i.e. you're a bigot also) but it might mutate as the appearance of the opposite (i.e. being a passionate civil rights supporter.) Either way, you are driven by the energy that was passed down to you. It is a part of why you would be attracted to becoming a civil rights supporter: you recognize the vibration of bigotry. Genetically, you still hold the bigot energy in your energetic system, but have chosen to redirect the energy in a different way. My father was an alcoholic for most of his life. Both my brothers drink freely. I monitor myself carefully. It's the same energy directed to manifest differently through conscious or unconscious choice. Different perspectives.

In this lifetime, if you were bitten by a big dog when you were a child, and you go into a panic when you see a big dog, you are still holding that energy in your energetic memory and defining yourself as someone who is afraid of dogs. If it was a big dog owned by a person of another race, it becomes doubly loaded for you because of the vibration of bigotry you are holding in your energy system. The two vibrations become one larger pool of energy that influences who you are and the choices you make. The genetic predisposition of bigotry and the life experiences of the dog become married into one larger experience.

Let's add a third possibility into the mix for fun. If, in a lifetime previous to this, you were unjustly treated, spoke up for yourself, and were stoned or beaten for doing so, you might find it more fearful to speak up for yourself in this lifetime for fear of retribution. So now we have an added layer of vibrations to an already loaded scenario. You get bitten by a dog (that you attracted by an initial fear from different race (which you hold judgment and dislike for because of the genetic vibration predisposition,) and you are afraid to speak up for your rights (because of the past life vibrations still in your field.) This can cause levels of confusion, self-doubt, and anger pouring into this one scenario in this lifetime. If these are not balanced in this lifetime, we will probably continue to drag them into others.

Ultimately, nature and nurture work hand in hand in the matrix of our vibratory lives. If we are consciously working with those vibrations, we can consciously choose to redirect the energy to more positive and healthy outcomes.

Let's go into a little bit more detail with basic energy principles. Atoms are the smallest piece of a substance that still has all the properties of the substance, but they are not just tiny balls of mass. They're made up of subatomic particles (protons and electrons, among others) that have some very interesting properties. From the diagrams of atoms we saw in school, electrons appeared to be little BBs spinning around the nucleus of the atom.

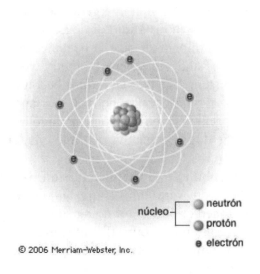

núcleo ⎡ ◯ neutrón
⎣ ◯ protón
◉ electrón

© 2006 Merriam-Webster, Inc.

26

In reality, however, scientists have learned that electrons don't have any dimension because they can manifest as either a particle or a wave. Electrons are particles when you see them and waves when you don't see them.

As a particle, electrons take on a distinct form. As waves, electrons move differently; they can travel through separate openings at the same time as a giant mass of potentiality. To help you understand this a little better, let me give you a simple example. Say you're sitting in your living room, which has two separate windows that are open. If a car goes by on the street, the sound you hear comes through both windows at the same time. The sound waves as electrons of potential don't pick a specific window to enter through. In contrast, if a baseball were hit at the windows, it would go through only one because it has distinct size and dimensions and gets focused more specifically. The electron as particle is specific, like the baseball. The electron as wave is non-specific, like sound.

Subatomic particles only manifest as particles when they are observed. If no one is looking at them, these particles act like waves. The reason this is so important is that this energy only manifests into something we can see, something in material form, when we are focused on it. If focusing on something brings it into material form, then not focusing on something will eliminate its material existence!

In this same way, we create our lives. By focusing on something (consciously or unconsciously,) we are actually causing the energy to manifest physically in our lives whether we focus on a great job, an illness, the perfect mate, or a terrible boss. The energy is materialized because we are focused on it. That focus directs the energy (consciously or unconsciously.) When we focus on losing weight, we are actually creating particles of weight. When we are focused on needing more money, we are creating particles of lack. In contrast, if you are focusing on fitness, you are attracting particles of health and fitness. If you are focusing on abundance, you are attracting particles of wealth.

This doesn't mean we have to neurotically monitor every thought and statement. The fear creating rigid control lowers the vibration itself! Just follow these two principles:

1. Only think and look at what you want in this life.
2. Know that when you tell the universe to send you something, it does.

Communication with the universe is instantaneous. Creation should be effortless and fun, as it is in nature. It certainly is in science.

Experiments in quantum physics have shown that in wave form electrons can actually communicate with each other instantaneously. Now this is pretty miraculous because even traveling at the speed of light the communication between the two electrons couldn't happen instantaneously. So the only conclusion that would allow this type of communication is that there aren't two electrons. It's the same electron reacting as a whole, not two separate electrons reacting at the same time, even though two electrons were observed. The key word here is observed. If the electrons only appeared separate when they were observed, but were part of one entity when they were not, then what we see as separate is actually part of one big wholeness! Like the dog bite and the bigotry, they become pooled into one human current of being. That one wave is broken down into separate waves because of our perspective. Our perspective defines how we choose to see the waves and, therefore, how they manifest in form.

Glass half full

 Glass half empty

We see the glass according to the truth we are vibrating in, but it is the same glass.

When we observe something (our bodies, our house, our car, or other people,) we are seeing the exact same energy, the One Energy, but manifested in different and specific ways. All of it is part of a whole energy. Source. We are part of this whole as individuals. We have simply defined ourselves differently so we can see ourselves (and others) as distinct and different.

The One, therefore, expresses itself differently depending on us: our perspectives and our choices toward creation. The One Reality is created from all of our joint perspectives pooled together. When those perspectives are redefined, so is the One. When the majority of the One sees Peace, peace manifests. No man is an island. We all contribute to the perceptions that create the One Energy.

All is one. Spiritual teachings and science concur: we are individual representations of the whole. We define the whole.

So how does this modern view of physics fit into your life? Well, if everything is energy, and we are all part of that energy, and things are manifested by our vibration, then focusing on what you want will cause it to manifest. You just need to be conscious of what you're focusing on, and the vibrations of intention behind your focus. For example, are you angry or happy when you focus on more money?

Again, perspective plays such an important role in the vibration. Two people can be focused on the creation of more money, for example. One person's perspective is that money is "evil" but he still knows he needs and wants to create more. The second person knows it's the choice behind the money that creates its worth and she needs and wants to create more. Both are focused on manifesting more money, but from dramatically different vibrational perspectives that can create different successes.

By focusing on what we want through higher consciousness perspectives, we actually attract and create particles of manifestation reflecting what we want! The same holds true if we focus on what we don't want.

The particles we create also exist in past, present and future times as well as in several dimensions, simultaneously. This is the quantum idea of the physics of particles. Most quantum physicists today believe the whole universe is actually a hologram. Put very simply, holograms are created by splitting a laser beam and bouncing one of the two beams off an object and the other off of mirrors. The result is a three dimensional image of the object that can be viewed from all sides, but has no physical structure. It's an illusion. Your hand can pass right through it if you try to touch it. If you've ever gone through Disneyland's Haunted Mansion, all the ghosts are holograms. To many physicists, so is life. The illusion of life changes drastically with the magic of perception.

It's important to understand one basic property of holograms—every part of the hologram contains all the information in the whole. So if part of the hologram is cut out, the remaining parts still retain the information of the missing part. Everything is part of the whole and the same as the whole. I only present this because you need to know that when you direct the One, you are directing all energy as it currently exists in your hologram: past, present and future lives, in all dimensions, all time and space, all levels. If information in one part of the hologram exists throughout the entire hologram, the totality of the lower vibrational energy must be included consciously. This work transmutes energy throughout your entire hologram and onto the collective whole.

You don't create energy; you only change its form. All the energy present today has been present since the Universe began. If you transform the energy within your hologram, the projected image changes. The core changes. Meaning if you change the core that makes up the energy you create your life with, your life will change and look different. It will have to be projected differently.

Remember that thoughts, beliefs, genetics and past experiences (including past lives) are energy. This energy creates your hologram. If you think you're sick, the image projected in your hologram is of a sick person. If, however, you believe you're healthy, then that is what manifests. It projects into your life. The Universe responds to the picture you hold. Beliefs are expectations made up of energetic pictures, which vibrationally create. That's why moving out of what's "real" and into what your dream looks like actually is more beneficial to manifestation.

Take, for example, the scientific research that has been done on how patients' beliefs affect their health. Let's look at the placebo effect. Patients were given a sugar pill and told that it was a great new drug that was going to make them well. Those patients often had improvements similar to or better than the patients who were given the actual drug. The placebo worked because the patients believed they were taking something that would make them better. They "pictured" themselves getting better. They vibrated at "I'm getting better." The radio station they tuned in to was the "I'm getting better" station. They were given permission to focus their energy on the cure, not the sickness. They allowed themselves to focus their vibration on wellness because something outside of themselves (a little sugar pill) gave them permission to claim that perspective and focus.

Multiple personality disorder is another example that supports our beliefs creating reality. Cases have been documented where one personality needs glasses, but another personality has perfect vision. One personality is diabetic, another isn't. Each personality has its own energy and is vibrating in its own beliefs and definitions. This perspective manifests as traits in the physical body depending on which personality is holding the perspective. That personality is projecting its own hologram. The one personality vibrates in the belief that he needs glasses to see; the other vibrates in perfect vision. If the physical ailment is based on the individual energetic perspective and vibration of the person, then it stands to reason that if you change your vibration, you change the physical manifestation.

That's what this work is all about. Change your perspective and you change your vibration which changes your life. It goes beyond thought. It is all about the energy in your hologram and how you are choosing to direct the manifestation of it. We've heard for years from different spiritual gurus that change must happen within first. Science now agrees.

Chapter 4

We Create Our Own Lives

THERE'S A GREAT AWARENESS IN our society today: "We create our own lives." Our consciousness is being reminded that we must take responsibility in the creation of our own manifestation. I believe the statement is putting a lot of us in confusion, fear, misunderstanding, and false expectation simply because we don't understand the energetic machinery behind the concept. We become frustrated when manifestation isn't instantaneous. We forget that healing is an ongoing process, a learning to become conscious process.

Through the perceptions that we hold, our thoughts are formed, our vibrations are created, and our world is manifested. Let's pretend we are children who are lost and trying to get back home. We look around at our options, and we decide that going right is the only way to get back home. Right is the way that seems to make sense. So we start walking and the perception is that we're going the correct way, but we never get back home because we perceived the wrong way to go, even though our perception told us it was the right way. When we don't get where we want to be, it appears that the Universe is working against us and keeping us from getting there. Ultimately, it's not the Universe at fault. The Universe supported us in the choice that we made out of our perceptions. It was our perception that was at fault. The discovery of our own limiting perceptions is the ongoing process of ascension.

The first step in truly manifesting what we want through co-creation with the One Energy is to consciously be aware of what perceptions may be leading us down the wrong paths. For example, if I go into an audition as an actress and my perception is that they always think that "I'm not right for the part," that perception keeps being perpetuated into my experience and my manifestation. My focus is on, "I want to be right," so my fear (vibration) is around, "I know I'm not going to be right." My fear from my original perception keeps me subconsciously focused on what I don't want, so I keep creating it. I don't create what I really want, which is to be right for the part.

Hopefully, my perception changes after several auditions. Hopefully, eventually, I discover that belief doesn't work because I keep not getting the part! The Universe is actually saying to me, "Dee, this perception doesn't work. This perception that they think you're not right keeps giving you what you don't want. Maybe you need to change your perception of how you are looking at your universe, so you get to the manifestation of what you want."

Ultimately, many of us are lost, and we're taking the wrong way and we don't know it. We're not creating what we want because our perceptions have directed us incorrectly, and we can't understand what we're doing wrong. Many of us don't realize this simple truth. When we don't get what we want, we fall out of trust, we fall into fear, and we say, "See, nothing I do works. No matter how hard I try, it doesn't work." It doesn't work because our perception from the beginning was incorrect. The perception needs to be changed first, so our intention can be manifested.

The Universe responds to our intentions, perceptions, and directions, whether they are conscious or unconscious. If I am holding the perception that I'm never wanted, the universe responds perfectly to that and creates that for me. In doing that, it shows me that my perception is not manifesting my desire. Albert Einstein said, "Insanity is doing the same thing over and over again and expecting a different result." If the results stay the same in our lives, we must start looking at our perceptions of the world and how those perceptions are affecting the creation of our world. That is an objective, conscious process.

The old patterns aren't working anymore. The belief that we have to force something instead of living in the true power of creation is antiquated. We were taught that the only way to create was to force and control, keep the fear, watch out for others, and make sure nobody was taking advantage of us. These are all paths leading away from "home." Now we must shift those perceptions into the knowing that higher vibrations, clear direction, and co-creation with the Creative Force manifest our desires from and with love.

We are continually challenged by the concepts of good, bad, positive, and negative. We're so ingrained in believing in the separation of energy into the yin and the yang. What we have to realize is that the Universe is always supporting us in whatever choice and decision and perception that we are choosing to live in. The Universe is always in a perfect dance with us. When we are able to move into calling everything good, then we are able to open ourselves to the perception that the entire world is rushing forward to support us in what we want to create. When my perception in the audition changes to, "Wow, all this feedback has been really good," then I can realize that the perception of "they don't think I'm right" is not serving me. I get to choose a different perception. Like the child going the wrong way, I get to choose to acknowledge that the way I picked is not the right way. I get to choose a more direct way, so that I can arrive at truly being home, and "being right" for the part. That responsibility is mine.

I want you to picture a field, an amazingly beautiful field of wildflowers, butterflies, birds, deer, and nature. It goes on as far as you can see. Up above you, below you, to your left, and to your right you are immersed in the middle of this holographic field around you. This is the field of all possibilities, of all probabilities. You're in the middle of it so you can choose which way to go. How many possibilities and probabilities do you choose to see? If you see weeds, if you see dead flowers, if you see thorns, your field of possibilities and probabilities takes on a whole different perception than the person who sees beautiful wildflowers and beautiful nature and all possibilities that can be created out of that. The thorns and dead flowers that we see are the fears of the things we want to avoid, but even those can be nurtured. Our perceptions of those things create how we maneuver our field of possibilities. If we feel stuck because we see no apparent safe path, that perception can limit us from creating one.

For example, many of us accept other people's limited beliefs regarding our success. If our path is created in fear—I want to avoid those thorns, I want to avoid feeling bad, I want to avoid the fears, I want to avoid being not right for the part—then our path becomes one of avoidance. Our perception is that we have to avoid life and control life to safely get home to the things we want. That perception keeps us in avoidance and subconsciously keeps our focus on things that we don't want, which creates them in our lives.

When we choose to walk down the path of all possibilities, with the perception that we can choose and create with the Universe the possibilities we wish to manifest, true manifestation is possible. Because the entire holographic field is available to us in all its possibilities, the choices and paths are never-ending. Creation is happening in every moment. Our perceptions drive our choice of the paths we see and focus on when we take responsibility for self and quit blaming the Universe.

Creating our lives is an ongoing process. It is an ever-expanding, ever-growing, ever-reconfiguring universal field. Healing, then, isn't a stopping point. The perception that healing is done, over, and completed with a quick sound bite answer once I have the secret is a false concept of how the Universe works. We are constantly in creation, constantly in choice. Like nature, we are always rebalancing self. Nature plants a seed, which grows, spreads, and plants more seeds. Sometimes the wind carries those seeds far away to be planted somewhere else. The path of creation is constantly being planted as we are walking down the path of all possibilities and consciously choosing our perceptions. When we move into the fear of the past or the expectation of the future, we move out of the moment of creation: now.

So many times, we say, "OK, I'm going to do it. I'm going to know. I'm going to do all the right stuff." But part of us is waiting in the wings to see if it really works. After two days, or two weeks, or six months, or a year, and our lives haven't shifted in the way that we "perceive" real shift, we give up. Like the child, we go, "Well, it must not be this way either." If we would just turn the block, we would be home, but we stop just short of home and decide yet again to take another false route away from where we truly want to be. We don't remain consistent. Creation happens when we are consistent in owning our new perceptions and holding on to these perceptions, *regardless of how the universe may be showing up* - in every moment. In every moment. Our energy must choose to step up to and into the perception of the highest possibilities and probabilities because manifestation responds to consistency.

We have all been taught that the world happens to us, and that we are not the cause of our world. So how can we own our consistency? Most of us are locked in victim consciousness whether we acknowledge it verbally, emotionally or vibrationally that life happens to us. We put it off onto luck; we put it off onto God, fate, bad timing, I just fell in with the wrong people, or my body's supposed to be this way.

Whenever we feel out of control, helpless, angry, judgmental, or judged, whether we call it victim or not, we are living in the victim consciousness and vibration. The perception that "shit happens" and we can't control it takes us out of the moment of creation. If you truly know that you are in co-creation with the Universe for your highest good, you are always living in the field of your own possibilities and your own creation. The world responds to your direction. If the world keeps on bringing you people and situations that lead you back to victim consciousness, you need to look at what perceptions are attracting those people into your life.

When the winds of good luck and financial abundance shift into what we perceive as negative, they are shifting in service to us, regardless of how it looks in the moment. If we are coming from the field of all possibilities and the perception that it's all good, we simply need to consciously and consistently direct the co-creation of our dreams and know that the Universe is rushing to enhance and create what we direct in our lives. To be true co-creators and partners with the one, we must, like any good partnership, do our part. We must say, "I know it's all good. I know all things are possible. I choose to direct what I want to be created in this life, out of the perception of knowing that the Universe is there to deliver all to me. I have planted the seeds with my direction and now I allow the Universe to nurture them and grow them and bear them in the highest way that the Universe can deliver it to me, which will be and is higher than any of the limited conscious thinking that I can create." Why would we ever be tempted to move out of this consistency, this moment of creation?

When we learn how to react differently because our perceptions have changed, when we can move into non-reaction or conscious reaction, out of the perception that it's all good, and it's all here to manifest for my highest good, all possibilities are open to us.

All of us know that oftentimes in our lives, we can take gigantic leaps in consciousness and in physical manifestation of what we want, which makes us say, "Wow, life's good." Then life seems to drop out again. We can make a huge move up in our consciousness and still repeat some of the old patterns on higher levels of our ascension journey. That's the process.

Whether it is beginning a new sport, a new relationship, a new business venture, or a new health regime, it all begins with a learning curve that starts at the most basic level and increases to mastery. We all have various perceptions that create what possibilities we activate in our field at each level. Even if those were from outside sources in our lives, we are still at choice in keeping them. Do we love ourselves enough to recreate our perceptions and increase our ability to respond to all possibilities? Can we choose to run the four-minute mile when no one else has? The point is once you get there, there is somewhere else to get to—in ascension AND manifestation. It's the process of life. One of the rules in that process is the following:

Energy is always in various states of moving, reforming, and redefining in different ways. Since we are the ones moving the energy, we are the ones creating from it! Do we want to move the energy into fear or into love? Into war or into peace? Do we want to move the energy into full creation or partial creation? In this very moment, creation literally is ongoing, waiting for our directions.

When we tell the Universe, "This is what I want, BUT this is what I believe," the Universe goes, "Huh?" It simply cannot get you back home with that muddled direction. We are vibrationally sabotaging what we want to manifest.

It may look like I can't move up, the money is never enough, or "they" won't hire me. In reality, my perceptions of the world and the beliefs about myself are thwarting my creation because those perceptions are still "I can't do it because of outside people and circumstances."

The truth is, I can't make anyone else focus the energy differently from their perspective. They must direct through their own choice. I must create mine. So I must always, only, focus on me. I may have to forgive people, forgive myself, or expand my comfort zone beyond what I can imagine, but I know that is the path of creation that manifests my desires. I will consciously shift and recreate my perceptions to allow the Universe to co-create with me all my good. I don't have a clue how it's going to happen. That's not my job. My job is to know it will, and claim what I want by directing it.

I love the Dr. Seuss book, *Oh, the Places You'll Go.*

"You're on your own. And you know what you know.
And YOU are the guy who'll decide where to go."

We all start off with that perfect knowing. Then, somewhere along life's path, we move into what Seuss calls "The Waiting Place." Most of us are waiting for everyone else to change. Playing against the self.

"I'm afraid that some times
you'll play lonely games too.
Games you can't win
'cause you'll play against you."

We sabotage our energy. The purpose of this work is to move out of playing against ourselves, which is ultimately playing against Source and the Universe since we're all One Energy. Instead, we move into play with Source, play that creates, and therefore creating the lives we want. We stay in choice, not reaction. In oneness, not separation.

In the moment that we enter into a reaction about anything, we choose not to create. Part of our energy begins sabotaging our focus. We have made a decision, which creates a certain vibratory state, and together they begin the creation process. It's usually not the one we want, simply because we are not consciously choosing the reaction. We are in reaction. When life gives you lemons, make lemonade. This is good advice. It's choosing the lemonade that creates higher vibrations of attraction that creates your manifestations. It is the conscious choice to remain happy. To call it good. To see all the possibilities. To create.

The only way we're going to get movement and change in this life is to stop blaming everything and everybody else. As long as we're pointing the finger at everybody else instead of ourselves, we are not taking responsibility for how we feel, for how we think, for how we direct our energy, for the choices we make, for recreating ourselves, for the perceptions we own.

The Drama of Healing

Bottom line, we are the only ones who have access to healing ourselves. We may, through our intention, use other people, such as doctors, pastors, or healers to help us heal, but ultimately, we are the only ones who do the healing for ourselves.

Many of us are kidding ourselves that we want to heal. In fact, we're hooked into the experience of trying to heal. There is excitement in, "Oh my God, I've got to find somebody to heal me. I've got to find somebody to save me. Am I going to be OK? I've got to look outside of myself for help."

The drama. Our world and society is really locked into—and feeding off of—the drama of "trying" to heal, "trying" to be abundant, "trying" to find a relationship, trying, trying, trying. We have a war on drugs, a war on poverty, and a war on terrorism. In an evening of TV, you can receive hundreds of messages about what disease you're probably going to get, what you have to take for it, and how you'll probably die from the side effects! This can't be the answer. We can't be this far out of control of our own lives. In essence, we're not actually looking for the answer. Because we're not looking within us. We're looking outside ourselves. The answer isn't "out there." "Out there" are the excuses we give ourselves to not heal. We're giving our power away to the fears and limiting beliefs of what WE DON'T WANT.

If you're blaming anyone else for how screwed up you are, you're giving your power away so you can't heal yourself. You are using your power to give your power away, by not choosing. Use that same power to pull your power back. You have to take your power back. You can't claim what you want while your perception is that you need assistance from the outside to get your power to create it. We are societies ingrained in giving away our power.

One of the primary places is our healthcare. Most of us have never been introduced to the fact that we direct our own healing. I have an incredible internist who has saved my life in many different ways over the past thirty years. I used to see him once a month just to maintain my energy and health.

Recently, I saw him for the first time in a year. At first, I was angry at myself for the relapse. If I am truly my own healer, then why did I need this visit? I surrendered to the fact that while I was on my path of self-healing, it was OK to get some help and guidance. I just had to stay in the knowing that he was helping me on this level of consciousness to heal myself. Ultimately, I know it is about my resistance to moving up in consciousness that created me having the flu. While I'm ascending, sometimes I need help to remember I heal myself.

Because of the fearful perception of death, we react with panic when our bodies tell us there is something to be healed. We react by giving up our power and grabbing at anything that might save us.

Take the cigarette syndrome: We smoke, but we don't want to smoke. We try the patch, the gum, the clinics, and hypnosis. If we are not conscious that we are the only ones who can shift the energy, we may be one of those that "have just tried everything and nothing works." You can see the perception behind the failed manifestation: it's not up to me. Someone or something has to do this for me, and the drama of trying keeps being perpetuated.

Anytime you unconsciously look to somebody for anything you think is not within yourself, you are giving away your power. You are giving your power to somebody or something else. You are saying, "You have power over me, power I don't have. I can't heal without your power." Until that stops, you're not going to have a lot of expansion, movement, or transformation in your life. Period. You've given away your right to create. Blaming is another great way of giving away your power. If you're blaming your partner, you're not healing yourself. If you're blaming yourself, you're not healing yourself. If you're blaming God, you're not healing yourself. Drama.

With blame, we lose our ability to respond, and therefore, direct, and therefore manifest. We stop working with our own energy. Our focus is on what we don't want, and we stop claiming what we do want.

Claiming is a concept you have to embrace to truly heal in any way, be it making money, finding a loving relationship, creating perfect health, being happy, or even knowing what you want. Claim what you want! This is mine.

Sometimes, you have to reclaim it. When I decided I wanted to refuel my career, I had to reclaim it. "I want to be a major actor again. I don't care if anybody else thinks it's too late. I don't care if my mom still thinks that being a doctor would serve the world much more. I don't care if it's hard. I don't care if I have lost my contacts. I want to be a major actor again! I am telling the Universe—bring me the creation of being an actor."

When you say, "I choose to know. I choose to believe. I choose to heal myself. I choose to get out of my own way. I choose to release all my own fears. I choose to do this for me. I AM creating my life," a myriad of phenomenal, universal forces come into play, working for you.

For example, years ago I told my mother that I wanted to be an actress. After I graduated from college and received my teaching degree so that I would (quoting my mother), "have something to fall back on," I said, "You know, I taught a year of high school, and if I don't go to New York now, if I don't start seeking my dream now, it's not going to happen." I loved teaching, but I knew teaching wasn't the end all and be all of where I wanted to be. When I said, "I want to go follow my dream and be an actress," my mother said, "Well, be an actress, honey, but stay in Kansas."

The subliminal message I received? "Dee, I believe in you on one level and I have a mixture of fear that you're not going to be OK. I am fearful you can't make it outside of Kansas." From a loving mother place of protection, I allowed her to limit me energetically because I chose to accept her fears, but something in me said, "You know, I can always come back. If I don't make it I can always come back to Kansas City. I can always teach and have something to 'fall back on.'" So I went to New York. I pushed through the fear, but it was always there—that fear of "what if." I had allowed it to become a part of my energetic expectation and perception. Part of me knew I was my only creator. Part of me sabotaged that with the fear that "life happens."

Many of the messages from my parents were a mixture of positive and negative, as they are for most of us. For example, we would all watch the Miss America pageant, and they'd say, "You could do that. You could be up there DeeDee. You can do anything you want to do. If you work really hard, you can achieve anything." That's the ethic that we all know so well. Work hard. Work hard and you can do anything.

So simultaneously, all the following became collapsed into subconscious confusion that affected my creative ability: "You can do it, you can be a Miss America pageant winner, but you should really get your teaching credentials to have 'something to fall back on.'"

Combined, all these messages equaled, "It takes a long time and you have to work really hard and if you're lucky, you get what you want, but don't count on it because it's not safe." Most of us are holding yes/no energy from a myriad of sources and experiences, and that creates a lot of healing drama.

If you're not conscious that many people's perceptions and circumstances direct your energy in limiting ways, and that fears and limitations are part of one big network that makes up your total energetic vibrations and perceptions, you are not creating your life. You are living theirs. Your movement forward has the wind taken out of its sails. Like the Little Engine That Could, part of you is saying, "I think I can. I think I can," and the other part of you is saying, "Be careful. Watch out. You're not safe. I don't know if you can do it. Maybe you can do it. You should give it a shot, but don't expect too much." It takes the power out of "Deliver this to me."

True power is creation itself. As Marianne Williamson said, "Our deepest fear is not that we are inadequate. Our deepest fear is that we are powerful beyond measure. It is our light, not our darkness that most frightens us. We ask ourselves, 'Who am I to be brilliant, gorgeous, talented, fabulous?' Actually, who are you not to be? You are a child of God. Your playing small does not serve the world. There is nothing enlightened about shrinking so that other people won't feel insecure around you. We are all meant to shine, as children do. We were born to make manifest the glory of God that is within us. It's not just in some of us; it's in everyone. And as we let our own light shine, we unconsciously give other people permission to do the same. As we are liberated from our own fear, our presence automatically liberates others." All great power moves into creation

Christ turned water into wine. Buddha performed miracles. Gandhi created peace in the face of the British army. Roger Bannister ran the first four-minute mile. Jonas Salk discovered the polio vaccine. Leaders from all walks of life back to Noah and the ark were all-powerful. They did not accept the limitations of themselves or the people and the world that surrounded them who said it couldn't be done. They did not accept the beliefs, fears, and the norm of society. They created higher perceptions. They moved into the power of creation that belongs to all of us. We are our own creators; we must not wait for anyone else. We must define ourselves and then create. We must intend, choose, direct, be happy, and keep our vibration balanced.

It's All Good

Again, it is a scientific fact that we are all One Energy and nothing is separate. If nothing is separate, we are individualized expressions of the One, and if we are One, we are Creation itself. As individual expressions of the One, we are constantly at choice regarding how we define our expression from the perceptions we are holding. One person defines his expression of the One as an investment banker. Another defines hers as a loving mom. A fashion model. A priest. Lonely. Happy. Jealous. It is our choice as to what perceptions we hold that creates us as defining and contributing to the One Energy.

The highest vibratory choices pool into the collective to literally shape the One Energy in higher vibratory ways. Our responsibility is in our choice. We are consistently at choice to perceive everything as good, to choose to perceive the world and all that happens in it as learning experiences along the path. The path is the very reason for it all. The path doesn't end. We keep creating it anew as we travel. Reach one destination, and we're beckoned to an even higher ascension. That understanding balances a lot of frustration.

Sometimes we get what we want in a different way than we are asking for it, and we move into the assumption we haven't gotten it. When it took me six years to conceive my daughter, it came to me in an entirely different way than I had planned and expected. I was frustrated, challenged, and oftentimes despondent. I felt that the Universe wasn't delivering to me. Everything I did "didn't work." I didn't know it then, but during that time, I was experiencing and being taught much of what I needed to create this work. The Universe was putting everything in motion to deliver in the highest way possible through love. I kept focused on what I wanted and kept creating, despite outside influences. I received my beautiful daughter as I was being schooled for bigger things. Ultimately, I could see it was all good.

Often, we also attract circumstances so we can test ourselves around how far we've come in staying in creation. Can I still hold my vibrations high and NOT go into reaction? It empowers us to experience that and gives us confidence to continue to vibrate in a higher place and remain in creation. For example, when I was hurt by this particular industry person, it took me twenty years to forgive and move on. When

I was challenged a second time by a good friend sabotaging me in business, it took me two months to forgive. A third test came when a family member was out of integrity regarding family finances. It took me two days before I realized, "Hey, I know this place. This is the same anger. I'm not staying here. I'm not lowering me with anger and judgment because they are out of integrity. I am choosing to call it good. I am consciously choosing to stay consistent in my beliefs."

Other times, the Universe is simply putting us in a place to serve OR be served. During a particularly vulnerable time in my life, I took a turbulent trip on a plane. The man next to me held my hand, comforted me, helped me laugh and keep my vibrations high. Recently, I got to be the one in service in exactly the same way with a fellow airline traveler. Helping her keep her vibrations positive kept mine in a high, positive state also. We all work together within the One Energy. It's all good.

Source Energy creates. You are part of that energy. You can't ever eliminate energy, but you can change energy. You can transmute energy, and we direct how that energy is transmuted. We're all defining our own energy in different ways. We're defining The Energy differently, but we're the same energy. Once we truly understand we are the same energy, we recognize our duty to create our individual energy in the highest way possible. The acceptance of this duty is the beginning; it is the acceptance that everything is created by you. You are power. You choose where to give your power when you choose your perceptions and reactions. You choose where to put your power when you consciously choose where you put and focus the energy you create with. As you create you, you create the world. Consistently. It's all good.

Accepting this opportunity will change your entire life. It is the power in your life. It will change everything you know about yourself and everyone else. It's the biggest and most important knowing that you can have in order for you to start creating your life today. If you separate yourself from the One

Energy, you have created an illusion for yourself. As soon as you limit yourself BECAUSE OF SOMEONE OR SOMETHING ELSE, you do not move forward in fully shifting your own creation because you have given your creative power away.

Sit for a minute and ask yourself to whom or to what situation you may have given your power of creation away. Did you lose your vision? Why? Are you giving your dream away? Why? Are you creating your life the way you want it? Why not? Did you give it away to another person? Did you give it away to the belief that you couldn't actually do what you loved and what you wanted to do? Or that you could only go so far? Where have you become a victim in your life by pointing your finger outside of yourself? Did you stop saying, "I am creating me, from this moment forward?"

Remember—we were given choice. We are the creative force that has chosen to define itself in a particular way. Which way are you defining yourself—victim or creator? "There are no victims, only volunteers." I say, let's not volunteer to be victims anymore. Let's move into our own creation and get transformational movement in our lives, starting right now. Like E.T., we need to take the steps to get back "home" into self-creation. This work facilitates that. Create your life. Trust that you are shifting energy even as you are reading. And remember, life is a process.

Vibrations: Walking the High Road

Chapter 5

Intention

INTENTION: THE AIM THAT GUIDES the action; an objective; meaning or significance.

The intention with which you create anything is vitally important to the manifested energy contained in the final result. In other words, the energy behind why you choose something influences the results. Direction and momentum start from the launch point of your vibrational answer to why you are intending to create anything.

As we know now, everything is energy. That energy is ongoing. All energy mixes and interplays with other energy. Thoughts and beliefs are energy. Ideas are energy. So intention, made up of thoughts and ideas, is also energy.

Think of it as the seedling that germinates into a great tree. Within that tiny seedling is all the information needed to produce the final product: the species, size, branch formations, leaf shape, and bark type. An intention is the same: all the energy in your seedling of an idea grows into every branch and dimension of your manifestation. The vibration of your intention helps determine the vibratory content of the creation, the final result.

The answer to why we have chosen to have a child, become a doctor, help the needy, or create a business is the beginning energetics of the core to our resultant creation. The "seed" you plant manifests in the clarity and integrity of your intention. I can best represent this with a personal story as an example. Years ago, I decided to add an additional class to my studio (my creation) because I needed to generate more money (my intention). I was already overloaded energetically, but instead of knowing that "God is my source," I followed what was now a familiar pattern in giving up myself to get what I need and giving up myself to help others and working myself to the bone to just have enough.

So, I created that additional class and it filled up immediately, but it was more difficult than my other classes had been. The energy was frustratingly low. None of my techniques to teach students to play with a high vibration were working as well. After having developed and honed much of this work, I sat down and asked, "What energy is holding my Wednesday class back? I want to know the highest limiting belief I can balance to move the class forward." The final statement was: "I don't know if I have enough energy to do this." Those were the exact words I spoke to my associate when I began the Wednesday class!

Like any creation, this entity of the Wednesday night class took on an energy all its own from my intention and vibration. I literally attracted people who were being challenged by the same issues I was. My vibrations of energy lack and financial fear perfectly matched many of the people I attracted to that class.

The implication here is clear. You create from your intention, and your life reflects the energy of that intention. If we bring the energy of lack, fear, anger, desperation, or any lower vibration into the intention of anything in our lives (businesses, relationships, family, or health) we begin creating from that energy, which gets delivered directly into the Creation itself.

Think about it: What intention are you now bringing into your business? To financially benefit or serve the world? Hopefully, both are combined in your intention: to truly want to serve while enjoying major financial reward. Do you want to help others in the highest way possible doing something that gives you joy or make a living in something you hate until you can retire?

We can see the effect of intention in our businesses. The intention and the worthiness with which you create your business affect everyone from the top down. Anyone who has ever been at the top of their business, the creator of their business, or the lowest man on the totem pole in the business, knows this is true. The people who are in charge, the people who set the original intentions of worthiness and perceptions create a whole stream of consciousness that filters down throughout the entire organization. Henry Ford created an empire with his perception, "If you think you can or you think you can't, you will always be right." He set the intention of success.

Intention affects our families. Is your intention as parents to nurture your children's needs or to insist they grow into yours? Parents who don't believe in themselves pass their intentions, limited though they may be, down to their children. Sins of the fathers pass down generations and generations and generations so that the same patterns keep being repeated. I often say to my daughter, "My good attributes: my love, my caring, my talent are yours if you want them. All my fears and all my limitations from generations of our family, let them go and create new perceptions. Let this be the end of them now. They are not yours to own." Families can go decades and generations repeating the same limiting patterns because their perceptions remain stuck. Until someone in that family becomes conscious enough to say, "This has been going on in my family for too long. I'm choosing something different," the perceptions keep limiting further generations unconsciously.

Another example is one of my best friends, who had worked in the movie industry for years as a respected, admired and competent Production Manager. He loved his work and people loved him. His intention in going to work each day was to have fun, turn out the best job at the best price that was possible, and to do his job well. He knew he was good and celebrated himself.

Eventually, he decided he wanted to move up. He thought he should be producing, but he didn't like producers, nor did he really have a lot of faith that he could produce. The Universe matched those vibrations. He received rejection after rejection, became bitter, and lost his joy. The energy behind his daily work turned from fun and high self-esteem to resentment and bitterness. The jobs fell away; the money dropped out. He was forced to declare bankruptcy. His "intention energy" had switched midstream, and so did the reality of his life.

It is important to understand that the minute we state our intention, we begin directing our intention to manifest. Obviously it behooves us to pick an intention that serves a large scope. Since the world is ever-ongoing, redefining, and rebalancing, the highest intention is to love. Stay in the intention of love—for yourself, for others, for the world, and for the Creative Force. Living in love is a valuable tool in manifesting what you want. You vibrate in the highest perspective possible as you direct for the One Energy from love. Intend love.

When we set our intention, it is the first step in directing our energy toward what we want, in directing THE energy to manifest for us. It is our focus on creation. If you are confused in any moment regarding smaller intentions, choose the one that feels closest to peace, bliss, and love—the higher vibrations to your "authentic self." Walk away from intentions that are fueled by greed, judgment, retaliation, or any other lower vibration.

It is our belief that we have chosen this lifetime to experience this process of ascension in embodment for the first time in centuries. We need to lovingly remind ourselves that it is a process, and the
process of choosing to change and redefine our limiting perspectives is part of what creates the quantum movement for the One. As soon as one person *chooses* to ascend, the vibration of the whole raises. When many choose, there is quantum leap change. As we challenge ourselves to redefine

our energy, we must love ourselves through the process.

We often need to ask for discernment or clarification around our intention. We get confused and lost regarding what is positive. For example, sometimes we move into lower vibrations that feel like higher vibrations because it feels good to get back at someone, or to be right, or to win at all costs. From fear, we jump into retaliation. It feels good in the moment because of the adrenaline rush. It feels good because we have forgotten the good of peacefulness and peace. It feels good because we are familiar with it. It is our Ego. We want to choose the lower vibrational power of the ego in the form of retaliation, judgment, war, and bitterness instead of the higher vibrational power, which is the true CREATIVE power in the form of peace, bliss, harmony and love. Keep your intention in the love boat. It will steer your course to the high water! Use the lower vibrations as a warning that you are going off course. They are a valuable tool in informing you of limited perspectives. Remember, it is a process of learning to choose differently to manifest creation and to be in conscious creation.

How Intention Applies to this Work

Your highest intention is to create the life you want while holding the higher intention of love for the good of all. Love is the highest frequency we can vibrate in. It is Creation itself. Love balances all energy.

Love + Conscious Creation = Manifestation

Here we have a bit of a conundrum. It's the old chicken and the egg problem. Which comes first, living in love (God/Buddha, all encompassing, all accepting, all allowing, all empowering, all knowing, peaceful and ever expanding) or having to ascend to even do that? If we all lived on secluded mountaintops in peaceful vibrations with no life challenges, the answers would be more obvious, but even secluded monks have limiting perspectives!

Again, we have some scientific rules to guide us in the process of this choice:

Everything is Energy.

You can change/transmute energy.

You have to do this by conscious direction, which includes the following:

1. The perspective you choose to hold in any given moment.
2. The vibration you choose to hold in any given moment.
3. Belief.
4. Your consistent practice of these principles.
5. Accepting all responsibility.

Even here, scientifically, you have to leap before the net really appears. You have to begin the journey a step at a time. Remember, it's a process. It would help right now if you stop and evaluate your perspective on trust. Are you willing to trust enough to begin? Most of us want guarantees that the goods we invest in are worth the price before we put the money down.

The Universe works in direct opposition to that perspective. It is asking that you hold the perspective and vibration as the creation you want. You are not waiting for the Universe. You are the Universe. You are your own creator. Can you trust that this is so and be the master of your own Universe? Do you trust the truthfulness enough to step out into creation and change your perspectives?

Self-trust is an important first step. We simply haven't learned it very well. We've never been taught that trusting ourselves with our own creation is really what it's all about. We haven't received what we've wanted because we didn't participate in the creation of it. We actually created what we didn't want by our focus outside of ourselves, so of course we distrust, especially in the Creative Force. And ourselves. Our manifestation hasn't appeared. We started to expect things not to be delivered to us. We have been holding that perspective. It's time to choose differently in our process of evolution.

That process is different for all of us.

Basically, the very definition of trust is that it needs no proof or verification. It is intrinsically a confident knowing of something. It is that intuitive feeling—that knowing beyond physical evidence.

And, sometimes, in the process of ascension, physical evidence is gratifying.

Looking back on the revealing truth of this work, I created 60-80 students to help give me physical evidence. I knew I was being led. I knew I was attracting new information. I just didn't trust why it was me receiving it! My students supported my need to have myself checked, to fuel my perspective that I wasn't enough. Then, so much evidence appeared in manifestation that I moved into trust that the work worked and it came through me.

Perhaps this can help you move through the fear of recreating a whole new mindset toward creation. Moving through the fear is uncomfortable, but it is part of the process of ascension and re-creation. Don't be afraid of your fear. Use it. Like your other emotions, it is a tool to unlock awareness.

At one point in my career, I did a film in Bulgaria. For some reason, I was terrified to go. I had never been to Bulgaria in this lifetime, so in this incarnation it made no sense. When the fear almost became insurmountable to the point that I was thinking of pulling out of the project, the Universe worked in a mysterious way. My daughter was cast in a small part. It was her first major film that she had secured on her own. I couldn't back out now!

I began consciously directing my energy to release and balance all the frequencies that were creating this overwhelming fear, which I couldn't even identify. I was able to peacefully make the trip, and yet even during my time there and my flight back, the feeling of fear surfaced often to alert me to be conscious to choose a different perspective. As I said, it is a life process of moving into empowerment as you see your life manifesting in a different, more balanced way.

I trusted the work enough to trust myself and the Universe. Trust your feelings. They are right for you. Some leaps are a single bound. Some leaps are practice for the final competition. What is important is your choice of expanding into ascension and love at whatever pace is right for you and whatever place you are in now.

Basically, you have to trust enough to begin. The truthfulness of this work will prove itself to you. You must choose to begin to heal. We are all fearful and feel the need to protect ourselves in the world. That fear keeps us from expanding if we don't move through it. Indeed, it creates more of the fear.

The basic consciousness of mankind today is, "I must protect myself from the things I fear." That is living in reaction, not creation. You don't create what you want from fear until you can listen to it. Fear is limiting and debilitating if you don't use it to grow. You cannot vibrate and tune to the "creation station" while your vibrations are tuned to the "victim station." Use your fear to create.

Setting a strong intention allows you to use and pass through the fear. It directs your energy and the Universal energy to focus on creation instead of limitation. It creates a specific plan: go here.

Intention to Live in Love = I create love for myself, others, my world, and my creation in all ways.

Unconscious Intention to Remain in Fear = I create fearful things in myself, others, my world, and my creation in all ways.

It is obvious, then, that intention cannot be compromised if it is to fully manifest your desires.

Love + Fear = Confusion. Limited direction. Limited creation.

Fear and love are opposite vibrational states. Opposite intentions. When you hold love and fear simultaneously, the vibrations become mixed and collapsed. The manifestation is affected by creating a lower vibration than pure love, therefore attracting less than you hoped for creation. We all know it is possible to love and fear at the same time. We love our children, yet fear for their safety. We love our world, yet fear for our safety in it and for the world itself. In doing that, we are mixing intentions. Which radio station are we choosing to listen to? Fear is tuning into the angry, judgmental, and untrusting music station; love is the happy, calming, and trusting music that lifts you into a higher place.

Life is the continual process of consciously choosing the higher motivational intention of love. When we are challenged, it is our most important choice to make. Finishing this book presented one of those challenges for me.

Six months before I finished this book, I had to force myself to claim the intention of completing this book. I had reached a wall. It's a wall that is very familiar to me throughout my life and in several different ventures. I would go so far and for unknown reasons that seemed out of my control, I would always hit that wall and fall somewhere short of successful completion. I first had to become conscious of that pattern in my life. I admitted there must be fears that kept creating that pattern. Then I had to consciously choose to set the opposite positive intention: complete the book with love in the highest way possible. Once that intention was declared, all energy began moving toward that intention. I was focused on completing the book. I consciously chose to love myself enough to allow the Universe to work through me and my fears. Every day was a challenge, but manifestation followed.

Sometimes moving forward means looking at and experiencing fears, judgments, and limitations that you're not conscious you are holding. Sometimes I had to be brave to know myself. Sometimes I put the book away for long periods. Then one day I would wake up and all my energy said,

"Complete the book." I was excited. The information poured onto the page. I was vibrating really high. Obviously, I finished the book. Love took me into trust that I would be guided to complete it.

Setting the intention created a willingness to realize all the energetic limitations that had been clogged in my energy that were preventing me from completing the book. When they surfaced, I embraced them as the gifts they were. I balanced my frequencies around them, raised my vibrations and life took off. Balancing the energy that is limiting you is simple. The next few chapters guide you through this process.

Sometimes the manifestation of our intention may not be what we expect. For example, let's say you are in a relationship and your intention is to create that relationship as honorable, communicative, joyful and respectful. Your partner's intention is to create a relationship where he can be controlling, deceitful, dramatic and manipulative. Obviously, these are opposite intentions. You are responsible for yours. When anything, such as marriage or business partnerships, depends on the pool of intentions of two or more, the intentions need to be in harmony. If they are not in harmony, they are in conflict. It's a bit of a conundrum because you have to keep the focus and high vibration on you and your intention. Once your focus shifts and becomes locked on the other's misalignment, you begin creating that lack in your life. It's challenging in a relationship that is faced with opposite intentions. We must vigilantly remember and identify this. Again, the challenges are being presented so we can heal something within ourselves.

Harmony = clear direction/high vibration
Conflict = muddled direction/lower vibration

In the above relationship, we keep focused on harmony. The partner will begin to shift or move on, but we have remained in creation of what we want: harmony and love. Hopefully, the bond is strong enough that each person wants to live in love for the greatest good of all, and what needs balanced in each other's frequencies is balanced. During ..... process, the intention is living in love and the direction for the relationship becomes focused and clear.

I can't change my husband's intentions. I can't change my daughter's intentions. You can't change your boss's. They are responsible for their own. Like perspectives, intentions are individually created, held on to, or changed. Intentions are affected so much by the perspectives we hold that the same intention can passionately seem positive to one person in the relationship and negative to the other.

From the parent who was suffocated by their own parents, allowing their teenage daughter her freedom to express and find herself is a positive, higher vibrational choice. Their partner, who was involved in a teen pregnancy that hindered their opportunities early in life, sees it from a whole different perspective. Too much freedom = trouble. Both are coming from the intention of loving and taking care of their child.

When the intention is clear that love is the highest intention, we become united in working together to serve that intention. What is important is that each holds their balance so they keep vibrating and attracting what they truly want: harmony, peace, love and communication.

So often our focus becomes about what someone else is not doing, the responsibilities they're not taking, and the opposite beliefs they have. We move out of love and acceptance and into judgment and control. Our vibrations fall. We move out of conscious self-creation so we can make them wrong.

Again, the challenge is to consciously bring ourselves back into the balance of love. Although it's an ongoing process, it is one that becomes more instantly accessible as we practice the intention of consciously choosing love.

As we grow and evolve, oftentimes our intentions need and want to morph into higher choices. Always be open to claiming a higher intention. You may have started out just wanting to do commercials and now intend to win the Academy Award.

Great! Allow that new intention to be born in love for the highest good of all, with work that moves and touches the world. Stay open to all the possibilities the Creative Force sends your way from your intention.

Ask yourself, what is the highest intention behind your healing? Take a careful look at the intention with which you begin each day. It is a vitally important step to finding the trail of breadcrumbs that will lead you home.

Chapter 6

Good Vibrations

IN ORDER TO MANIFEST WHAT we want, we have to ask for what we want, while we are vibrating at a matching frequency. Most of us, quite frankly, are confused about what that means. When you are at zero point, in balance, the teeter-totter evenly aligned, you are vibrating at a matching frequency. You are open to all possibilities. Being neutrally in the moment of creation allows for all creation to manifest. Neutral means without fear or exciting expectations. Neutral. That allows the Universe to align to the vibration of all allowing. Most of us have interpreted vibrating at a high frequency as always having to be happy, always smiling, always being in love, always needing life to be okay. This is authentically not where most of us are. Most of us go up and down, in and out in life. That is the normal state of energy—always rebalancing. To believe we must live 24/7 in a Pollyanna state in order to create is a false premise. One that is causing a great deal of angst.

To be in the neutral place of choice, we must be able to choose. That isn't possible when our happiness is still dictated by how life "looks," because we are still allowing ourselves to respond to the Universe instead of choosing the response in a positive way, no matter what the Universe sends us. We stay in reaction instead of creation, which doesn't allow us to stay in choice. We fall out of balance into lower vibration.

When we are able to perceive that, even at our worst, we are worthy and divine, we stay in choice. Then we start moving into the self-love that allows ourselves to shift our perspective into "it's all good" and remain detached in neutrality and creation. Once we raise ourselves up into our worthiness and our knowledge of our worthiness, we are able to see others as worthy also. Then our perception of true worthiness is really born. We move out of the limited definition of worthiness, which is now our ego, which presents itself in the world as, "See I'm better than you are."

Most of us are under the misunderstood perception that we are starting to manifest or that we are choosing to manifest what we want in this moment now, like we have to begin something new. In reality, we have been manifesting from birth. We have never been not manifesting. Being alive is manifesting. Breathing is manifesting. Creating anything is manifesting. Now, our desire is to move into the self-love of worthiness so that we actually begin choosing what it is we manifest on a conscious level. When you vibrate in the higher perspective of it's all good, I love myself, I love the world, and I love others, you actually vibrate in that higher perspective. It allows you to choose to see things differently, instead of merely reacting to life. It's more about allowing the journey to unfold and choosing to stay balanced on the path. Ultimately, it is the process we're moving through that is the gift. It's the process in the next step that we're taking that is actually our manifestation. Neutral keeps the vibration in allowing.

As we're looking at what's coming into our lives, if we call it "bad," our vibration drops and our manifestation becomes limited. We can't see the possibilities. If we call it good and see it from the perspective of the glass half filled, we are embracing everything that comes into our lives with the perspective that it's a great opportunity to experience something. It's in that knowing that you stay in a higher vibration and attract what you want.

Let's take a moment to discuss what "higher" and "lower" vibrations really are.

"Lower vibrations" are vibrations that stem from REaction to an outside source; they are the frequencies of fear:

depression, anger, hatred, apathy, jealousy, despair. You can "feel" lower vibrations. They are heavier. They keep you out of creation and in victim consciousness. They can be useful to us because they can be the force that pushes us into creation of what we want, but only if we use them as tools to move through them and back into flow. These lower vibrations become the catalysts for your change in perception. Again, coming from the perspective that all is good, we know that these emotions are serving us, and that helps us to move into the higher vibrations and even newer perceptions. Perceptions that enhance our happiness.

Lower vibrations zap your energy if you choose to remain in and wallow in them. They keep you from taking action toward balance and manifestation because you are FOCUSED ON WHAT IS MAKING YOU FEEL BAD OR THE EXPERIENCE OF FEELING BAD. We need to use them to kick our butts. Why is this happening? Why do the patterns repeat themselves? What perspectives keep creating this? Use those lower reactions as tools to recreate your perspectives on creation. To put you back into control. Neutral. Good vibrations.

Merriam-Webster's definition of control is to check, test, or verify by evidence or experience. So ultimately, we are always in "control" of our lives if we remain conscious and proactive with ourselves.

Higher vibrations resonate with action, not victim consciousness. They are powerful because they put you into the control (check/test/verify) of your own belief system. Higher vibrations are the path of re-creation. They move you out of the lower vibrations and into the honesty of our limitations and false perceptions. It is the choice. It is the owning of the perception that it's all good and I am creating me in every moment through my ability to respond to the information given to me. Your creation responds to the vibrations created by your perceptions, so your creation will always match your vibration, stemming from your perspectives and reactions. You can't say that you want to be healthy and be focused on sickness in an attempt to manifest health. You can't claim you want abundance if your entire focus is on lack. If I keep looking at my big butt, it's not going to get smaller! So, "I'm not worthy" is not a vibrational match with, "I create what I want."

High vibrations are easy to identify. They are playful and loving, peaceful and giving. They are never ego-based, although to others they can look self-consuming. Oftentimes, when we do what is for our highest good, it can look selfish. We are simply never taught to love and honor ourselves in worthiness, so most of us can't identify what worthy looks like. When we put our soul's needs first, society often reacts in a negative, accusatory way. We are supposed to put others first.

A friend of mine finally gave her husband a loving ultimatum: get a job and help support this family or we need to separate our energies. In essence, she was not only serving herself, but she was serving him. She was serving him by no longer enabling him to not reach his potential any longer. Her vibration was one of love while knowing she needed to be honored. The fear the ultimatum brought forth created the catalyst that opened up discussion for further growth and partnership for the couple because THEY TOOK STEPS TO MOVE THROUGH. That allowed them to create more balance, so they could see what they both really wanted: a successful marriage. We simply can't create higher vibrations unless we serve ourselves! Energy serves itself. It serves us. It is our life force. The process is about putting ourselves first on the higher level and then serving others because we have raised our vibrations.

Here's an example. My neighbor to the right of my property really lives on the adjacent street. His backyard borders my front yard. Months of demolition and reconstruction had deposit boxes lining the front right side of my house, making parking difficult and my house unsightly to visitors. I said nothing.

But after the work had been completed, he knocked on my door to tell me his son was going to park there and to please keep it available.

I felt the rage pop in me. Immediately, my warrior came to the rescue with all the usual rebuttals: it's a public street, we'll see who gets there first, blah, blah, blah. As soon as I balanced my vibration about the parking space and recognized what I wanted, from my higher perspective, was to be peaceful and happy, I let it go. The result? He parks there about one day out of the month. I just let it go. As long as I was holding the vibration that I have to be right, I actually create him wanting to come back and retaliate so that his ego can show me that he's right. Neither one of us ultimately gets what we want: peace. Everything serves us. I chose the perspective that peace served me more than "I have to get what I want" and to trust the Universe is serving me.

Living in high vibration was the most difficult aspect for me in this journey. For so long, I had to take care of so many people and make my own way that I had forgotten how to play. I had to learn to serve myself by having fun, taking more time for me, getting massages, and speaking up for my needs. I had to learn to love myself first. I needed to trust that all was coming forward to support me.

We all need to shift our perspective back into trusting the Universe. That includes trusting our Self. Loving our Self. Good vibrations.

Even the bible tells us straight out: "unless you change and become like little children, you will never enter the kingdom of heaven." (Matthew 18:2 NIV) I had lost my child. My responsible adult was proud that she was stressed about money, proud to be carrying the load, proud she was "so tired I can't go play tonight." I was vibrating in that boring adult place that doesn't create because I had lost my objective balance.

Children expect good. They say what they need and what they want. They order from the world and expect to receive. I'm always striving to find my child, to lighten up. To play again. To let the dishes go or visit the beach or sit in the backyard. To trust I'll get the toy. It is still challenging for me. It feels irresponsible, and for me, that is still difficult to accept.

My husband, on the other hand, is a child. He loves to play, to be silly. He embarrasses our teenage daughter to death! He makes us laugh at the stupidest things. He had difficulty taking that fun into the real world. He thought he had to turn off his fun when he went to work. Turning off his fun was like death to him, so he pushed work away from him, or he was not happy in the work that he did. He had to integrate life and fun from the opposite perspective of mine. I had to learn to bring fun into my responsible world. He had to learn to bring responsibility into his fun world. We attracted each other perfectly as mirrors of unbalance.

Once we begin vibrating in a balanced frequency, the world begins manifesting our direction and then we simply allow ourselves to receive.

We do have to take action and keep our vibrations high by recognizing the Universe serves us. If we hold firmly in our childlike expectation, direction, balance, and vibration, creation appears. Without taking that action first, all other efforts are partially sabotaged. In ascension, we recognize that better things happen when we allow them to unfold. Then we are living the direction, the higher way. We have learned that we already know. We're already in co-creation. Then the statement, "Even before you ask, it is delivered to you," takes on its true meaning, and we vibrate attraction.

Visualization

Visualization is an age-old art where one "sees" in his imagination the positive scenario he wants to create. He "sees" (visualizes) the positive scenario exactly how he wants it manifested. Coaches do this with athletes—see the ball going into the hoop, the receiver catching the ball.

Visualization as a whole is only a part of the process. When you visualize, if you visualize peacefully and in the knowing, then the visualization absolutely helps you create what you want through focus and vibration. If you visualize from the intention of, "I'm going to make this happen. I'm going to sit here and I'm going to go into this meditation because they said that's what I have to do to create what I want," then you're working against the Universe vibrationally. You're pushing and manipulating. Not loving.

In essence, any scenario you run through your mind can serve you if you consciously use it to inform and guide you. If you find yourself immersed in a fearful scenario, AND YOU CHOOSE TO RECREATE the fears and perceptions around them, those fears have served you in recreating with the Universe your vibration because the choice brings you back into balance.

If we have angst or anxiety or feelings of, "Oh my God, is it going to happen?" you are not in the belief. You are out of balance, not at neutral, and the fear vibration dilutes the manifestation. You have to allow yourself to move through the fear, not deny it. Not live in the vibration of "what if " for the future, but live in the moment of now and create.

Knowing

When we take off for a destination, we know where we're going and have a plan how to get there. We set our sights and intentions on where we want to go. The accepted perception is that we're going to get there. We accept we are going to arrive. That acceptance and knowing keeps us balanced. Just like ordering a meal in a restaurant. We have no doubt in our minds that we're going to receive that meal. So we order it and we let go. We do have the intention of what we want, and we're coming from the perception that it will be delivered unto us. Knowing. Balance. Good vibrations. Most of us don't apply this to life. We live in hope it will "be OK" and life will "be good." We don't live in the vibration that it is always good. We live in the hope we'll be "lucky."

Lucky and knowing are vibrational opposites. Lucky suggests risk and uncertainty and a force outside ourselves that might come in and deliver us! Knowing is a state of grace that encompasses all other needs. Knowing is Creation itself.

Our enigma is choosing to stay in the knowing even when—especially when—it appears we should abandon ship. Most of us believe in God when life is good and fall into "why have you betrayed me?" when things don't go our way. Authority figures also take us out of our own knowing because "they are smarter, more educated, more opinionated" and they should "know."

True knowing cannot come from your mind. It is an experience you live in: a steadiness of peaceful assurance that you have inexplicable proof within yourself of the perfectness of each moment.

My greatest example of this in my life is the journey conceiving my daughter. Everyone told me it was impossible. All the "experts" who "knew." But I had a greater knowing. It was, simply, going to happen. There was no doubt. Only knowing. Knowing is manifestation. When we are in balance, we can choose to know. Then all the meals arrive, and the car reaches its destination.

Chapter 7

Forgiveness

FORGIVENESS IS AN INVALUABLE TOOL for holding our vibration. It is greatly misunderstood. The purpose of forgiveness is to aid the self in balancing its own frequencies, so it can move into the flow of all creation. We are never victims because we are always creating. Therefore, the choice to forgive is actually a powerful statement of release. We let go of our judgment and move back into the flow of energy by raising our vibration. If everything happens to us for a reason, the people and circumstances we are allowing to block us, are actually gifts, if we choose to shift our perceptions. So forgiveness is another tool we can use to keep us from remaining stuck in our lives. It allows us to move into a higher vibration. Some people don't need to forgive. They can simply let go and forget. The point is to MOVE ON.

The reason most of us stay stuck in non-forgiveness is that we love to wallow in what has happened. Not only does it give us an excuse for why we "can't" create, it offers us a wonderful sense of community with our fellow victims. It binds us together as commiserating partners of stuck, non-creational life experiences.

In reality, choosing to know we are our own creators gives us the power to transmute whatever frequencies created the need to forgive. It just takes true consciousness in perceiving the lesson. How much we perceive to forgive equals the breadth of what we need to move through within our own energy. The biggest gifts I have ever received in this lifetime were the numerous people close to me who sabotaged or hurt me in some way. The amount of love I was able to experience in forgiving them, and the freedom it created in my life, truly taught me about self-creation and the choice of self-love. I moved into the energy of loving myself so much, I had to choose to flow. Whenever you are stuck, you are stuck creating where you are. If you are in anger, you create in anger. If you are stuck in lack, you create in lack.

I want love + I'll never forgive/move on = Being stuck.

Why do you think the Bible says "Judge not?" (Luke 6:37) When you move into judgment, you move into focusing on the negative, which lowers your vibration and halts the creative manifestation. The person you are judging is not affected—unless they are retaliating and judging you in return. You keep feeding the very animal (judgment) that will ultimately devour you.

There are two components of forgiveness:
1. Being responsible for our own energy and not trying to control another's.
2. Knowing we don't really need to forgive because all is here to serve us. It's all good.

When we know that we are always living in the choice of self-creation, we know that another's actions don't have to affect us, and we also know that their "stuff" is coming forward to serve them. If you are judging someone, it is your energy coming forward to alert you to heal yourself.

Most of us move into the judgment that creates the need for forgiveness due to fears of worth, wanting to be heard, or wanting life to be "fair." We mistakenly believe that it is other energy that must be dealt with. In truth, anything that has to do with energy that is not yours is not yours to own, worry about, retaliate towards, or heal.

So basically, forgiveness is a decision we make so our own energy can flow and create. It is the letting go of what is keeping you in a lower vibration. That can be achieved by just forgetting and moving on, by realizing things happen for a reason and seeing the greater lesson, or the actual act of forgiveness itself. Whatever tool works, the intention is to let go, flow, and create in a higher vibration. Then we move back into actually creating the world—individually and globally— that we desire. It is again, the ongoing process of ascension. What helps one, helps the world.

Some might think it is a selfish decision to choose that all that happens serves us all, all the time. It is, truly then, "all about me." It isn't a convenient truth that we choose when it suits our ego. It is the truth we live from.

So often, our judgment of the world is actually a participatory experience. If our child, partner, or co-worker is involved in energy that we perceive to be damaging or "negative," we immediately choose to participate in saving or rescuing, instead of witnessing how they are being served. And how you are being served. Stand back and be the independent spectator in simply looking at the situation.

If a third party, such as a friend's friend, or another kid at school, or, globally, a foreign country—any energy that doesn't directly affect your life—is involved, it is simply not yours to judge. It is not within your energy field to deal with. If we are plugged into reaction, we are being called to heal what is being accessed within ourselves. What does it bring up within you? Heal that.

The media is an obvious example of how we are bombarded with information that is not ours to own. Constant fears of disease, danger, and impending doom are thrown at us continually, and it is simply not ours to own. We are invited to witness and judge each other in everything from courtroom dramas, reality wife swapping ventures, and childrearing abilities to wars, injustices and politics. We have become a society who is trying to experience their own power by judging other energy we don't even know! Then we wonder why our own lives are falling out of creation. We need to answer only to our Self.

There is a story that exemplifies this perfectly. Two monks were on a holy trek to a mountain. It took one day. During that day, from dawn until dusk, they were not to talk, or interact in any way, with another person, or even with one another. They plodded along quietly for hours over hills and meadows. Finally they came to this stream. Standing there was a frail old man.

"Please sirs," he pleaded, "Could you help me cross this stream? I am old and feeble and cannot do it alone." The one monk began to move ahead without acknowledgement, but the other stopped him. He handed his friend his satchel while motioning to the elderly man to climb on his back. He then proceeded to carry him across and deposit him safely on the other side.

Hours later, the two monks finished their long journey, the one monk seething the entire trip since the incident at the stream crossing. Finally, at sundown, the silence could be broken. "I don't believe you did that," the second monk chided. "I don't believe you broke the vows. You are disgraced. You have no discipline." The first monk stood there smiling patiently, which incensed the second monk even more. "Why are you smiling at me?" he commanded. The first monk waited a moment, smiled, and replied, "I put him down at the stream. You've been carrying him ever since." Like the second monk, those of us who carry around the need to be right and are unforgiving have a much longer and unhappier experience. Do not hold on to what does not serve you. Live in the flow of life. Move on. Move forward. Forgive.

So the intention in forgiveness is to forgive because you want to keep yourself moving forward. Christ didn't say "turn the other cheek" because he was a wuss! He was moving on.

My life has been filled with the lessons of forgiveness. It is undoubtedly my biggest challenge this lifetime. My childhood with my father was a consistent challenge of forgiveness.

I felt unloved and abandoned. When I made finalist for homecoming queen, we were all supposed to be escorted by our fathers. He couldn't promise me he wouldn't be drunk, so my teacher escorted me. I won. Later, my mom would tell me that, "Daddy was in the stands watching." It really didn't matter. Bottom line, the bottle was more important than I was.

I loved my daddy. He was fun and creative. He could make me feel special and beautiful and cherished like no one else. He would dance with me in the living room when we watched "Hit Parade" on Saturday nights. He could make Christmas more fun and special than anyone else I've ever known. He was a child at heart.

At one point, after his suicide, I remember talking to my youth leaders, Bill and Donna Robinson. They were angels that Source sent directly to me. "Deanna," they said, "You've got to know everyone does the best they can do. We're all here to learn." They helped me forgive the crap and celebrate the good so I could begin to move on. It is a lesson that I would use many times in my life. My forgiveness affected my vibration, which affected my happiness.

As in my example, most of what we need to forgive is far into the past, which keeps us in the past: how we perceived life as a child, all the added "injustices" over the years, ways we couldn't "fight back" or "be treated fairly." As an adult, it is our ability to respond to a new choice that allows us to see a bigger picture. We are able to see others' limitations and circumstances. We are able to even see the gifts we may have gotten from perceived hardships. We are more able to let go because we, too, have now made many mistakes. We must choose to want to see these new perspectives.

Forgiveness depends so much on your perception of how to forgive. To truly forgive, you must release your own energy back into the flow of love. Allow yourself to see their incapability and forgive yourself for carrying it around for so long.

Forgiveness isn't a requirement for staying out of hell. Hell is staying in the stuck energy and not moving, not flowing. Thus the term "hell on earth." When we attach the vibration of guilt, as in "you better forgive or...," we bring our vibrations even lower. Remember, the greatest intention is to love. Loving yourself by moving on enables you to get back into the flow.

As an adult, I can see that my father did the best he could. He was simply too damaged and incapable of healing. I am able now to separate his drinking from his love for me. They are separate unto themselves. I choose to remember the love and the good things. It serves me better. I learned from the drinking and lack of responsibility what I do not want in my own life. They are tools I now use to consciously create what I want.

From hurtful, deceitful romantic interludes to major business retaliations that devastated my career, I learned the difficult lesson that I had to forgive in order to live more fully. For me. Not them. I had to move on to live the life I want to create.

I have forgiven my best friend, my daughter, several partners, family members, many business moguls, myself and God, so I could move into the understanding that just the concept of having to forgive God suggests that Source would choose to do anything that doesn't serve us. That immediately goes into blame, we become victims, and we move out of our power to create. We forget we are the Source we are blaming. We forget all happens to serve us. There is nowhere in any religion that the higher power asks for forgiveness, because all of creation is good. All is in service. When we can truly understand that concept, we move on. Each time I acknowledge the good, I move on.

It's important to know who and what is keeping us stuck and use forgiveness as a tool to move on if needed. Let's face it, there are big things like suicide and small things like a slap in the face that can bookmark energy blocks in our systems.

Big or small, they can halt the flow if you continually wallow in the victim vibration of them. You know when you have released what you have been holding because your energy expands, opens and flows again. You move into gratitude because you see the bigger picture. It may not be instantaneous, but the process of flow and creation has been ignited.

Letting go allows us to reenter a place of choice: a place of love special to all of us. It has nothing to do with loving that person. It has everything to do with being in a state of love. It's a rainbow, a child, a pet, a song—that individual experience where we just simply know love. Consciously intend to be in that vibratory experience as you let go, and begin to see the power of peacefulness in your life. Then true, conscious creation can begin.

Chapter 8
Gratitude

GRATITUDE ISN'T SOMETHING YOU GET. It's an experience you move into. It is a state of being. You can't manufacture a state of being. It is authentic.

There is so much talk these days of "living in the attitude of gratitude." It is usually connected with the how-to manuals of manifestation, which tell you that you need to live in gratitude to create.

Knowing what we do now, we understand that vibrationally that makes sense. When you are filled with gratitude and awe for life you are vibrating at a higher frequency.

That is authentic gratitude: being so filled with the thankfulness of life that you feel lifted up. It is not lip service. It is a state of grace we are blessed with as we move along in our process of ascension.

The question I receive most in my workshops is, "How can I be thankful when I don't have anything I want?" – career issues, not enough money, illness, relationship problems. The answer is it's almost impossible because when we're pretty far down, authentically being grateful for what we perceive is lack, is blasphemous to our energy. We're simply negating a physical experience we are living. The only place we can start is by wanting to be grateful. Wanting to eventually move into that state of grace.

Wanting to find the smallest focus to begin. Being alive isn't it. Frankly, when we're really far down we're not thankful about being alive, but we can usually move into, "I'm thankful I want to be better and happier." Some of us can move into the birds singing, appreciation of nature, or love for an animal, a child, or a song. We have to be able to focus outside of our pain.

I remember doing a healing session in my backyard with a man who was truly despondent about life. I let him vent and express, and we sat there quietly for a moment. All of a sudden the birds everywhere burst into song. It was as if someone had ordered a feathered symphony just for us. "Listen," I said to him, "aren't the birds beautiful?" He raised his lowered head and said, "I didn't even hear them."

What had filled me with gratitude and awe hadn't even been able to enter his consciousness. Twenty years ago, someone helped me hear the birds. It is the process of life—the process of letting go and recreating our perceptions so we can move into authentic gratitude of being filled up.

Pretending "as if" isn't authentic. Gratitude is the result of moving into and choosing higher vibrations so that your perceptions shift how you see yourself and the world. The grace of gratitude is a marker for vibrating in a higher consciousness. You can't force it. You can intend it.

If we truly call everything that happens to us "all good" and look for the personal gifts of ascension offered to us, more and more moments of gratitude are possible because you are willing to see all as good. We are able to move into thankfulness for all that is sent to us. Eventually, when we truly master effortless flow through acceptance, we move into living in gratitude as a way of being. Part of that is knowing you are exactly where you should be in the learning, wherever you are. You are never a failure. You are successfully experiencing your process of reawakening. That is a prerequisite energetic acknowledgment in conscious creation.

Living in gratitude isn't a starting place. It is the realization that choices and reactions move us into higher vibrations that allow us to move into gratitude. To pretend to be thankful is not authentic. To think our way into thankfulness is not authentic. To be filled up with the experience of gratitude is when we know authentically we are Creation itself.

Choosing
the
Conscious Path

Chapter 9

You Direct, Source Responds

WHENEVER I USED TO WALK into my daughter's room, she was on the computer. I would like to think that she was studying that much! But no. She was always "IMing" someone. I finally asked her what that represented. After a dramatic roll of her eyes and the familiar "Oh my God, Mom, you are so ancient," she replied. "Instant Messaging."

Instant messaging. A way to communicate instantly and specifically with one or more persons. Immediate communication.

Without being conscious of it, we have always had at our disposal the most direct vehicle to IM Source: I AM. Each time we proclaim I AM anything, it is sending the message to the creative power that we want what we just stated. We are actually directing Source to create our statement as directly as we IM our friends to meet us in a certain place, at a certain time. Our direction to Source regarding manifestation is that specific.

When we say—or feel—I AM anything, we are communicating specifically with the co-creative power in the Universe. We send out a message, and the reply is sent back. It's a complete circle of manifestation. This is the most important concept to own regarding co-creating with Source, as part of Source. Source responds to our clear direction— CONSCIOUS OR NOT.

For me, this was the point of understanding that opened my eyes and introduced new perspectives of creation into my life. I had studied and acquainted myself with a lot of energy work, as I have mentioned previously. Authors like Wayne Dyer, Caroline Myss and Neal Donald Walsh filled my reading time. Visualization and meditation were a part of my daily ritual, but I was still struggling. In a fit of anger and frustration one day, I proclaimed I was tired of trying. I wanted answers to how we could heal ourselves, and I wanted them NOW.

How the answers arrived was so unspectacular that I can't honestly remember how they were introduced into my consciousness. Like most of life, the turning points come quietly dancing into your consciousness in hopes they will be recognized. For me, it was through a book called *The I AM Discourses*. It was the information that made it possible for everything else to work.

There are several discourses in the *I AM* series. Basically, they are discussions and teachings of ascended "masters" such as St. Germain, Jesus, and Michael. They were mostly written in the 1930s and have that dated, somewhat religious (although non-denominational) phrasing that drives me crazy. I usually pull away from exploring anything stylistic. Even Shakespeare is hard for me. Embarrassing for an actor!

So it amazed me that I could not put this book away. There was some knowing in me that there were answers here. The answers to my questions. I think I finished it in two days. When I revisited all the marked and turned back pages, they all referred to the same concept.

You must direct Source.

You are always directing Source whether you know it or not.

Source is always responding to your direction.

For me, this was an unbelievable concept. It was, quite frankly, almost blasphemous to me. I have to direct God? Who I am? No way. I had always been taught that I had to humble myself before God. It was all God's will, and it didn't matter what I wanted.

I read all the passages again. It felt like truth to me— freedom. I felt like someone had just opened a door that had been closed for a really long time, and on the other side was MY LIFE. I began trying on this new concept in my daily living. All I could do at first was direct without directing: if it's your will, if it's OK with you, if I'm worthy. All my old teaching. Slowly, I moved into really saying what I wanted. I want to be thin. I want to have money. Then I made the enormous jump to give me this. Give this to me please. I was still not at all energetically committed to the direction.

On the third reread of *The I Am Discourses*, I almost fainted. How could I have missed the section that said, "You ARE Source." So, in a sense, I was directing myself? Huh? And then I remembered my Bible School teachings. I was made in the image and likeness. These things and more we're all going to do. It all started congealing.

I AM Source defining Source as Me.
I have to direct Source to define itself—me.
All energy is Source. Therefore, I must define my energy in
    co-creation with other energy.
The direction = the process = the manifestation.
It was an awakening of indescribable proportion in my life.
I was no longer helpless.
I was no longer a victim of the world.
I was no longer blown by the winds of whim and
    happenstance.
I was a co-creator.
I had responsibility.
I had to choose.
I could create and recreate my life.

That realization, quite frankly, had never been presented in my life. I began practicing. It was most definitely a new comfort zone, one where I was striving to remain consciously in choice and creation. I am still in the process. The process is

85

the I AM itself: always redefining, enlarging, expanding, and understanding into other levels of awareness.

Since I have been living with the new awareness, a myriad of information is attracted to me daily because I AM ALWAYS ASKING FOR DISCERNMENT AND HIGHER INFORMATION. I've been introduced to more science than I care to even think about.

Science is confirming, from its point of view and within its own language, the very same concepts. Those scientific realizations are being made available (and understandable) to the general public. Consciousness is changing because the exploration of these truths are being introduced everywhere.

My life is changing exponentially during this process of redefining my perceptions about my role in co-creation. My health has improved, my finances have improved, my business relationships have improved. I'm happier and more centered and a lot less fearful… most of the time.

For me, the I AM is our IM to the Creative Force. We are instant messaging our direction to Source for the creation we want. The Creative Force IMs back immediately, even before you ask because we all know what we really want, and we are it.

Understanding and knowing the concept of I AM is a basic tool for this entire work. Without it, well, the work just doesn't work! It's like trying to ride the roller coaster without going up and down. It's an integral part of the ride. It is, actually, the ride itself. The concept behind I AM—that we direct energy— is the basis of why it's so huge for me. Any other tool that opens up your consciousness to the truthfulness of co-creation will serve that purpose for you.

Every time we say I am…, we are directing the Universe/Creative Force/God/energy to manifest what we are saying, and it listens to your feelings as much as your words. Basically, the I AM is knowing, unconditionally, that we are all part of the One Energy, and therefore, are the One Energy at the same time. It is "the Force" from Star Wars. It is "the power of prayer." Most of us simply don't have this consciousness.

Think of it as a ladder. We are all climbing up into a higher awareness of consciousness. We're all here to learn specific things in our journey, and therefore, all the rungs of the ladder are special and unique. They are serving you on your ascent. We can each be happy on the rung that is serving us now, as we each direct and co-create in our own individual different ways. What I need to learn on rung three may be entirely different than what you need to learn on rung three. What's important is that we are co-creating to learn by our intention and direction to do that. When our perceptions hold that it's all good and we're exactly where we should be, then we move into the strength of how can I and out of it's not possible. The I AM becomes a tool of consciousness. The I AM, to me, represents limitless possibilities when you have the courage to direct what you want.

Whether you work with your own intuition, Spirit Guides, Ascended Masters, or Source itself, it makes no difference. All are One Energy. Whenever we declare "I am," we are IMing a direction to Creation. We're exercising our responsibility. We're sending out and expecting guidance back. We're not praying to someone "else" out there; we are co-creating with the All. The work enables us to realize we are one with Source and have the benefit of all the energy and guidance in our lives. We are not alone because we are not separate. We are IMing ourselves.

If you feel a division of yourself from this energy, it is simply the ignorance of the mind because it is a fact. We all "know" this Oneness. We are it. We have simply forgotten. To fully create our lives we must move back into the knowing that we are the Creative Force, individually defined by the focus and direction we have chosen. We direct the definition of ourselves we have chosen ANYTIME we say, "I AM." Once that is done, it is imperative to remember that the Creative Force must, through its power, deliver our direction. It cannot implement its power without our direction. If we are not focusing and directing the energy consciously, we are directing it without knowing it—with our hidden fears, false beliefs, and limited perceptions. Because Source does not judge, the IM of your I AM is created any way it is focused. When we move into Divine Love and direct Source with intention, manifestation happens.

We must state with authority and power what we want, KNOWING THAT WHEN WE DO, WE DIRECT THE CREATIVE FORCE TO MANIFEST IT. And it does. Again, anytime we say I AM (anything) we are literally directing the Creative Force to manifest for us, as us.

To get a sense of the power of that statement, take a minute to ponder how many I AM statements you've made in, say, the last 24 hours. For example:

I AM tired.

I don't want to go home. (= I AM in conflict with home.)

I've got to lose weight. (= I AM too fat.)

I never have any energy. (= I AM a person with no energy.)

I AM bored.

I AM always broke.

I don't have enough money. (= I AM without money)

There's no one out there for me. (=I AM a person who can't find a relationship)

Because we are in constant co-creation with the Universe, we are always getting what our focus is on, albeit oftentimes it does not match "what we want." Because we are in ongoing co-creation, we must be especially conscious in the process of life and expansion, constantly reevaluating our perceptions. As Proust said, "The real voyage of discovery consists not in seeking new landscapes but in having new eyes."

It's Not Necessarily the Words

There are so many signals we send to the Universe as part of our "language" which direct and focus the energy. We can IM with no verbal declaration at all.

For some people, the words they speak are one of the most powerful tools they own. The commitment and understanding behind the words is a powerful tool of creation.

For some, like me, their emotions are their main communicative tool. My daughter chides me that I'm an actress because I simply can't hide anything that I'm feeling.

For many of us, our dedication to upholding other people's values, beliefs, fears, and limitations speaks louder to the Universe than any words.

There are a myriad of tools to be used in conversing with Source. Most of us share many of them in our dance of communication. What is imperative is the process of becoming more and more conscious of what you are holding and putting out. That is how you IM. Remember, the high vibration of balance allows choice. Sometimes the discernment of how that looks in life can get tricky.

Ever wonder why bad things happen to good people? To understand the importance, again, of how intention, balance, vibration, and direction interact, let's look at these examples.

Take Elizabeth, the favorite mom on the block. She does everything for her kids—drives them everywhere, is room mother, and volunteers for all their activities. "Hey," she says, "it's really for me. I'm with them, can keep my eye on them. I know they're safe." So what appears to be actions for her children are really defined by, "I AM a mother who doesn't trust her kids and who doesn't know her kids are safe in the world." That energy attracts lower vibrational fear, fueling what appears to be positive action. Her intention is vibrating from a lower place. She is literally IMing fear.

I know I was challenged with fear during my daughter's middle school years. I was "afraid" she was falling into the wrong crowd, afraid she was making the wrong decisions and she wasn't going to be a "good girl." The more I focused on those fears, the more I attracted things that fed my fears. Teachers warned me that maybe I should discipline her more. Parents called with concerns. When I brought it up to Gaby, she got defensive and emotional.

When I began looking into my own perceptions, I realized most of my fears had to do with me! If she's not responsible, what does that say about me? If she's not a "good girl" (by my mother's definition) how does that reflect on me? Do I fit the definition of "a good mother?" As I moved out of needing to be defined by what my daughter was, and consciously made myself focus on my own energy, things turned around. Sometimes miraculously. Quite frankly, if I hadn't experienced it, I couldn't support this work with the commitment to the I AM.

Over a period of time, Gaby's grades began improving and opportunities began opening up for her. Her relationship with herself grew stronger. As I looked more to myself and my own balance and healing, she began taking more responsibility. It is clear to me now that I was trying to control her so my definitions of "good mother" could be fulfilled. I didn't want to redefine my own limitations. That is why so often pain and suffering seem to be a part of the equation of healing. They don't have to be, but often they are the catalyst to make you realize the perceptions you hold are no longer serving you.

I have a friend who loans everyone money and takes care of people at her own expense, and who often runs short herself. "I just like to help people," she says. "When I help people, I'm happy." This seems to be a high intention, except that she is giving up herself. She is not taking care of herself as well as taking care of others. Right now, she is saying, "I AM a person who has to give up herself to take care of others." On the airplanes, they tell us to put on your own mask first. When we honor and love ourselves first, our actions are fueled from balance and are strengthened. The complete circle of giving and receiving can complete itself, and everyone is taken care of. "I AM a person who is balanced and honors myself while honoring others."

So we must be conscious. Many times we are directing the Creative Force to produce WHAT WE DON'T WANT. And we don't know it! Most of us are doing this unconsciously 24/7. That is why we are only getting part of what we want and a lot of what we don't. Remember: we are given choice. We must choose how to direct the Creative Force, so it can fully manifest what we want. Whenever you say "I am," you are doing that.

Think of it in simple terms. If you tell a child to bring you the stick on the other side of the lawn but to not cross the grass to get it, the child doesn't move. She can't. She doesn't understand how to give you what you want. How do I get to the other side if I can't cross the lawn? The directions are canceling out the possibility of movement.

That's what most of us are doing with the Creative Force every day. Our intention is, "I want to be a certain weight," and then we IM, "I'm so fat" or "I want to lose weight." The Creative Force is saying, "Hey! I'm confused. I need more specific direction. I am receiving the vibrations you don't love yourself, you are claiming you're fat and you want to lose weight. Clear up the direction."

How this confusion shows up in life is you lose a few pounds but not enough, or you can't stick to a regimen, or you lose it and gain it all back. You get the picture. Basically, there is a whole lot of resistance going on! Getting what we want is easier when we understand that it takes clear direction, high vibrations, balance, and creative perspectives in the process of our lives to keep us in the flow. Through our living and learning we can balance the blocks, beliefs, and fears, which are all energy, that are keeping us in lower vibration. Once those lower vibrations are balanced, we move into higher, lighter, joyful vibrations in our co-creation with Source. Ultimately, we transition to experiencing ourselves as Source.

The final jump is absolutely knowing you're Source. Aren't we all? It's all One Energy! Then, vibrating as Source, we direct the manifestation of our intentions for the highest good of all. When you say I am, remember you are directing Source, and you are IMing the Universe and yourself to give you a specific output in your life.

Good Vibration

You remember the phrase, "Ask and it will be given to you?" (Matthew 7:7) "Ask" in Aramaic, the original written language of the Bible means "to request, to demand, lay to charge, or desire." That is vibrationally not what most of us are doing when we are IMing our desires. Most of us are asking from a place of pleading or sublimation, from a place of unworthiness.

We have forgotten that all is One, that we are God, and so we define ourselves as limitations of God. We create separation where there is no separation by sublimating ourselves energetically. We grovel: "Gee, if it's alright, and if it's ok, and if you think I'm worthy....I would sure like you to create this for me." "You" and "Me" create separateness when there is only One Energy. And this keeps us in the pattern of vibrationally following the beliefs and perceptions of our parents, grandparents and their ancestors, who were also taught lack, limitation, and fearful perspectives of separation. Our IMs keep defining us in those ways.

The problem here is two-fold. First, we're not clearly directing the Creative Force (US) to give us what we want because we don't feel worthy. We need to direct: "Give me this. This is clearly what I want I'm directing this to be created now." Secondly, when we separate, we vibrate in victim consciousness and not victor consciousness, in ego instead of authenticity, in desperation and not clarity. That manifests as confused direction to the Creative Force. We are sending the message," I AM a person who wants this, AND I AM not worthy to get it." How, then, can the Universe deliver?

Basically, we have to create the new perspective and knowingness that all is in service to us because all is One Energy. Everything that happens in my life is coming to me to serve me in learning something about myself, so I can shift myself into the manifestation of what I really want through my conscious direction. The second thing that we need to own is the perception that we are Divine and truly worthy. It really doesn't have anything to do with self-esteem and how we feel. It's the knowingness that we are truly the god that we are reaching out to, the Source that we're reaching out to. The Universal Love that we are talking to is us. I AM Source.

"Who we really are" is the definition of worthy. It has nothing to do with what you think or who you think you are. It goes beyond thought. It is your beingness, and your true beingness is Source, and Source is love. And worth. And balance. Therefore, you, in your truthfulness, are also these things. "If I'm worthy, give this to me," is not a clear vibrational direction. If we don't understand the process, if we don't know that we're worthy, we don't really know what we need and what we want because we're in fear of asking for it or even envisioning it. We're stuck in the limitations of this lower level plane.

When our vibrations and our beliefs are in conflict, such as, "I want it and I don't want it because I don't know that I'm worthy," we're not in the balance of our true Self, and the IM of I AM less than God is sent.

Unclear, weak vibrational matches to your direction show up in a myriad of ways. You get a partial response, maybe a little bit of movement. You might even get some or most of what you want, then you lose some of it and fall back to where you started. You see, energy follows a pattern until it is redirected from your perspective. You hear us all lament to ourselves, "Why does this keep happening to me?" Well, it keeps happening because energy has to move. Energy keeps moving and without a clear direction, it keeps repeating the same patterns of movement because we have not chosen to redirect it.

How many of us keep going into the same relationships and creating them the same way with different people? How many of us in our dreams and our aspirations keep getting to the same point and manifesting to the same level and then things fall out on us again? That's a pattern, created from the same perceptions and expectations. That pattern has to be consciously redirected from a new perception, so the manifestation actually can complete itself. We consciously choose to ask ourselves, "What perceptions am I holding that are not allowing the manifestation to complete itself? I direct my energy to balance this. I choose a new perception of manifestation." We shift from "I AM a person whose life doesn't work" to "I AM a person whose life always works."

Always, we get tripped up by our own inner limitations. For example, as I was working through my blocks about worthiness, I found myself represented by certain agents that limited my potential with the same beliefs I held about myself. As I moved up in my own knowingness of my self-worth, I attracted agents that held higher beliefs in my potential, also. As within, also without. My energy was being mirrored in the world as it shifted in me. The Universe always comes forward to perfectly match what we are asking it to match: our perspectives. Our IMs. If I believe I can only have so much, I will attract the people who will perfectly create that for me, until I am ready to perceive myself and the world as a place where I am worthy and part of the One and can have it all. Then, miraculously the world seems to shift.

We need to shift our perspective to see ourselves as worthy. Until we love ourselves unconditionally and honor ourselves as the god that we are, as the One that we are, we keep running into walls about the clarity of delivering that message to the Universe. Our job is to simply and clearly, in the highest level of creation possible, claim, "I am god, I am one with the One. I AM Creation. I have been given direction to create everything in my life. I create love. I create manifestation. I create completeness. I create the knowingness that I am worthy of everything because I love myself so much as the One that I give myself everything that I wish to create in this world. I AM these things." Then I let that go and I move into the trust that the One (that I am) will deliver to me, unconditionally, in a higher and better way than I can ever imagine. I direct. This is what I want. This is what I wish to manifest in love and in worthiness. Bring this to me now. Create this for me now. Then I turn it over to the Universe for the most imaginative creation possible.

These places of confusion that are created by our limited perceptions keep creating the patterns in our lives, not only for us as individuals, but for our societies as well. We become directly responsible for the manifestation of the world that we're living in, because we are constantly putting our vibrations into the pool of the One. If we say we want peace, but simultaneously define ourselves as a society or as a people who don't believe they can have peace, we are pooling that all together into the One Energy, into the collective, into the society. So if the majority of the people in the society are defining themselves as not worthy of peace, the society itself must be defining itself as not worthy. The sum of the parts equals the whole. I AM a country who is divided regarding peace.

The confusion for most of us lies mainly in these three points:

1. The I AM is not an affirmation, a mantra. Manifestation doesn't appear because you do an exercise. It is the beginning of the co-creation of what you want to manifest. It is claiming your intention. A good director gives specific guidance with the intention of creating the cohesive whole of his vision.

    *   He begins by knowing what he wants.
    *   He is passionate in choosing this creation.

- He co-creates with his actors what he wants his final vision to be by lovingly guiding them to a specific outcome.
- He allows the actors freedom to arrive at that specific destination while finding it through their own creativity.

As any good director, we are co-creating with our cast, the Universe and Self, lovingly saying produce this, passionately involving ourselves in the production, and allowing the Creative Force to bring its unique creativity into the manifestation. It all starts with: I AM doing "this." Come on board, Universe. It's going to be standing room only.

2. Remember, this is a process of re-knowing yourself, and sometimes our timeframes aren't realistic. Perhaps we need to move into the experience of being worthy to receive what we're claiming, and we're just not vibrationally knowing our worth. Often we begin to question and doubt, confusing the Universe with our own lack of direction. Many of us simply have a false timeframe. The Universe won't deliver until it is in your highest good, but in our sound-bite society we want it NOW!

We are under the false perception that if we are instantly gratified, we must be doing it right, and if manifestation isn't immediate, we're wrong. There is no right or wrong. There is only the process.

None of the great accomplishments in my life came in accordance with my timing. I thought I'd get pregnant right away. It took me six years. I thought it would take me ten years to "make it big." E.T. happened in two. I thought once you had made it, that was it. I can honestly say I've "made it" now three times. I didn't want to do a TV series, but I wanted my career back. The Universe brought me a great series. It only lasted thirteen episodes, which led to doing feature films again. Mysterious ways that the Universe creates! I've gotten everything I've ever wanted (except a Broadway show), but never the limited way I had envisioned.

Don't give up! Hold to your visions, keep directing. We are so conditioned to have to know and be guaranteed the results so we can keep the faith. We have it backwards! Keep the faith to create the manifestation. If there are hidden perceptions not allowing you to keep the faith, find them! Create new ones that serve you. Live in the I AM.

All that realization of consciousness and the "stuff" we have to move through to get there raises our vibrations and allows us to ascend. Energy must expand and grow or it becomes stagnant. Vigilantly encourage yourself to hold on, keep the faith, and not fall back into how you've not created before.

3. A third factor that dissipates manifestation is our fear of not being humble. That was huge for me as I have shared with you. Who am I, we ask, to direct Source? Our religions have taught us that it is blasphemous and egotistical, that Source is almighty and we its lowly servants. Yet, when Christ turned water into wine, he was directing the energy to manifest his command. He also stated, regarding his miracles, "These, and more, shall you do." (John 14:12) It is a clear statement of permission. We were given choice. It has been appointed to us to choose. To choose is to claim a direction. In choosing, we direct.

Be powerfully humble by knowing we are the director. The Creative Force is the creator, but we work together because we also are the Creative Force. Source is waiting for direction to manifest for us. Tell it what you want! I AM _____.

How to Formulate Some I AMs

I often joked with my students that Source is standing on the other side of the door, waiting for us to knock (demand) so it can open the door, and we keep standing on the other side saying, "Gee, is it OK?"

Ultimate Direction

Direct Source to create what you want, but don't make it so specific that Source can't use its imagination to bring you an awesome delivery. For example, let's take the subject of relationships. After working with hundreds of clients, some of the major attributes we want to co-create in relationships are:
- Someone who respects and honors me
- Open, honest, fun
- Takes responsibility for his/her part of the relationship—financially, morally, sexually and energetically
- Willing to grow as a person
- Perfect health (a lot of us forget that)
- Shares the same interests
- Is stimulating
- Lives in love

You can see how these are looking at relationship frequencies that encompass broader ideas than just physical description. It is a clear, yet broad enough description that the Creative Force can manifest your direction in a myriad of creative ways.

Most of us would agree that someone with these characteristics would make a pretty fabulous mate, but many of us get so involved in "the look" of a relationship on the physical level that it is impossible to create what we want, or we get the facade and none of the important stuff. For example, this is one woman's list of important attributes for her perfect relationship:

- Taller than me
- Dark hair
- Rich (and what is that definition?)
- Nice to me
- Drives a nice car
- Likes to do sports
- Is good in bed

I think it's pretty clear that the focus here is—gee—a little more mundane than the first. Remember, what you direct, you manifest. So if this great guy comes along with blond hair, is he even going to get noticed? His appearance lies outside of the image. It could prevent him from even being seen. When you are truly in the energy of giving and receiving, you are in co-creation with Source. Source has always been working with you, giving you constant information and guidance. Therefore, we can trust that everything that is delivered to us is good and is guiding our process of consciousness. We then allow Source the creativeness of limitless manifestation.

Create the energy of the perfect mate, and they could look like Yoda and you'd think they were gorgeous. Seriously, aim higher. "I AM a person who is attracting a mate with the following attributes: (insert your list.) I direct all energy to create that for me." Remember, all energy includes your energy. Then let Source do its thing. You'll be amazed.

One of my personal examples is my comedy series, Sons and Daughters. I announced to my class, "Next year I want a series with great people, great material, and I don't want to have to audition for the network to get it."

A few months later, I walked into an audition for an improvisational comedy show. I almost didn't go. It was the furthest idea away from how I thought the Universe might deliver as you could get. It was pure heaven—the whole experience. Source created it in a greater way than even I could imagine. Now, as I look back, I realize this was my first conscious IM with Source. This was a beginning place of working with Source. This was the first time I consciously realized that I claimed, directed, let it go, and manifestation occurred—better than I could have "imagined" it. It was a huge shift for me to look back and see all the pieces in the process of my life that led to that moment: the energy training, the six years trying to conceive, the forgiveness work, the power and duty to direct, and the willingness to let go and trust the partnership of creation with the Universe.

I AM a person with a harmonious, fun series.

You see, I didn't specify which network, producer, or time slot. I claimed the important parameters. I should have left the money up to Source, too! Your job is to claim what you want by consciously using the I AM as your IM. Source will create it better than you hoped. Remember: I AM = I am directing Source to manifest my desire. I AM Source. I direct my own creation. I AM Creation! I claim it. I keep focused on it until manifestation.

The Universe is begging you: "Tell me, tell me, tell me only what you want." I want this body. I want this much money. I want a healthy, happy, sexual, and loving relationship. Only state what you want. Then you are claiming, I AM a person who has, I AM a person who is, I AM a person who does, I AM a person who makes, and you direct the Creative Force (you/Source) to bring you those things.

There is nothing we can't do in conjunction with the Universe and I AM energy. When you claim I AM, you direct the Creative Force on all planes: mental, physical, emotional, spiritual, chemical, cosmic, and dimensional. You direct the I AM to balance everything in the physical field, the mental field, the emotional field and the spiritual field. You direct the I AM to balance all frequencies within your body, mind and soul. You direct the I AM to continually lift off all negative or limiting energy that you may be holding. You direct the I AM to integrate all parts of yourself for the highest creation in love.

You direct the I AM to balance for all diseases, for all viruses, for all bacteria, anything that you may be holding anywhere in your energetic system that causes dis-ease. Anytime you are claiming I AM you are directing the I AM to balance the frequencies to bring you what you want in the highest way possible for the good of all.

Let's look at another great example that happened to one of my students. She wanted an agent, but didn't want to hop through the hoops to secure one, so she claimed it. I AM an actress with a great agent who is powerful, gets me out, works well with me, and is in integrity. Then she let it go. She came to assist me with one of my healing workshops and ended up helping a circle of people to do some work. In the circle was a casting director. He loved her and set her up with three meetings. She signed with an agent within a week. WOULD SHE HAVE GUESSED THAT'S THE WAY IT WOULD HAPPEN? No, not in a million years.

Life is meant to be easy and effortless, unless you don't believe that. Claim it: I AM my own creator because I AM IMing clearly and directly to the Creative Force within me.

Being Conscious

We have to be conscious of what we're saying, feeling, expecting and thinking to powerfully IM. Most of the time we're not. We keep claiming what we don't want. Unconsciously. As your vibration raises with the use of these tools, you become more conscious because you have different perceptions creating different views, and you don't need to deal with the same minutia. We are in a different consciousness as we move up. It becomes a game.

For example, on a daily level, many of us wake up and claim, "Uh—I am so tired. I don't want to go to work today." What Source is hearing is "Create me as tired and someone who doesn't want to go where I need to go to do what I've chosen to do." OK, we all have a few mornings here and there. That might only create a resistant day, but if it is a continual occurrence, you better believe you are setting yourself up. Be vigilant about what you're IMing. It is vital to realize that Source will not interfere in your direction—conscious or unconscious. It will simply manifest. There is no judgment, no right and wrong. There is, simply, direction and manifestation. It's job is Creation. If we get up tired, we know that's not what we want. We want energy. "I AM full of energy and excitement for this day! Yippee! I am IMing you, Source. Show me the energy."

I AM = God?

By stating I AM we are saying that we know that this encompasses all greatness, all creative energy, no matter what it's ever been called, anywhere, anytime. It is all-inclusive. It is the One. We have limited the I AM in our conception by having to put a name on it and putting it into separate and varied religions. The I AM defines the greatest energy of all, the creative energy of everything. It is Creation itself. So know that when we are directing the I AM we are directing everything inclusively. Not something outside of ourselves. What we're really doing is choosing and directing our expansion of energy and our definition of our expression of the Source we are. Source, being energy, is always expanding as energy. It expands through us. We are here to expand into the greatest energy possible: I AM Source. Source is all. We are here to expand into the all, to define ourselves as the greatest definition of the One.

Let me take a moment to explore why the term "I AM" is so powerful. It is because we have limited the concept of "God." We have put the God energy outside of ourselves and attributed all levels of limitation, judgment, fear and guilt around this powerful image. When we use the term "I AM," it includes ALL energy—every vibrational frequency existing.

I also found, for myself, that using a new, all-encompassing term helped me to lose a lot of the false moral baggage I was carrying. Over a period of two years, our work used several statements that aided in balancing our "permission" to direct. We used the following and several others until we were actually able to embrace ourselves as the One Energy:

I believe I can have God in my life.

Our frequencies are God energy.

I allow God to give and receive in my life.

Even today, we are led to realizations of how conceptually we are still holding on to separation. Again, the process of recreating frequencies of separation into wholeness is the journey itself. We are consistently being challenged to remember we are love. To always live in love. To be love. For Source is Love, the highest creative force of the Universe.

When our intention is to sincerely create the life we want while holding the higher intention of love for the good of all, and you direct using I AM, it is NOT POSSIBLE to create anything but the highest choice for you, others and Source. Because we have been given choice, we must know that what we claim is created in our lives and world. Source/Love is the principal of all life. Each person is an individualized, conscious, and active part of the One. Consciousness is always subject to direction through the use of free will.

Source can only act through you—by your conscious direction. If we separate ourselves from that creative power, we give ourselves an excuse for not taking the responsibility for our actions. We IM that I AM a victim. If we know that Source is us, and we are all responsible for the One, the label of God, Mohammed, Buddha really becomes immaterial. By thinking creation is outside of our responsibility, we don't control our thoughts and feelings, and we unknowingly feed and direct the One toward what we do not want. Manifestation occurs according to our focus. Our focus directs the energy where to create. We must take responsibility, for ourselves and for the world.

Sometimes this can be tricky. For example, you are stating (claiming) constantly that you want a successful business doing (insert yours here). You are ready to do this! You want people to loan you the money, find you the space, and get started. Except nothing happens. You don't take action, although you talk about it a lot. No one solidifies anything for you. You run into walls at every turn.

This is an example of how the silent IMing is at work. You are professing loudly, "I want this," while energetically claiming, in some way, "I don't," or "I'm not ready," or "I can't really do this," or "I never get what I really work for." So I can't take action. Again, along with the direction, it is the vibration you are holding with your intention that creates the manifestation. If any of these factors fall out, the result is sabotaged in some way. "I'm going to say I am ready, but I'm not, so I can't take action," still equals I AM NOT READY. The results speak for themselves.

World Vibration

There are tools everywhere in our day-to-day world that are serving us: radio, TV, film, print, and the internet. The media forces us to become more conscious of our world and ourselves. The very frequencies we want to raise are right in front of our eyes: sickness, war, fear, and revenge. It is very clear how we are IMing as human beings. The media is serving us by sticking it in our face so we can say, "Enough." There always comes that point when the higher consciousness takes steps to move out of one vibration and into another. When we consciously choose to make that movement upwards, then we lift our vibrations to a higher frequency. Remember, that attracts other higher frequencies to match it. Each of us must start with ourselves. Our I AMs affect the world. Each self, through the vibration of frequency, joins other like selves in energy. Two become two hundred, become two thousand, become two million and on exponentially.

The tools of negativity serve us to shift this way, if we choose. Like cable television, the Universe is always offering us many choices. What are we choosing to tune in to vibrate with?

Be conscious of what you are "watching" (focusing on.) Anytime we watch or listen we are casting a vote of choice: I want to focus here. We must choose to be conscious in the awareness of the myriad of negative messages (IMs) that we receive from our world and how we process those messages. Those are valuable tools in creating your life. Do the messages lift you up vibrationally and empower you, or plummet your vibrations and weaken you? Are you joining the vibrational pool that accepts that "one out of every three people gets heart disease" or are you consciously directing yourself to declare, "I AM health?"

When many of us can remain conscious and use this tool of negative energy expressed to us on a daily basis to support us choosing higher consciousness, the Hundredth Monkey premise could theoretically lift the Collective Consciousness overnight! It's the bombardment of the negative messages that is the Energy pressuring us for change, pulling our attention to wake up! The negative becomes positive when we choose to respond consciously as an individual or a group.

The principle is the same for all energy: the Universe responds to the IMs of vibration from our frequencies as individuals, families, groups, companies, countries, and solar systems. Our ability to respond with conscious choice redirects our energy and affects energy outside of ourselves by resonating and activating similar vibrations. As a pebble thrown into the water, energy ripples out to affect the whole.

We are consistently affecting our world and its vibration by our own individual choices. It is true: no man is an island. Energetically we are One. There is no separation.

Oftentimes, we become despondent when pondering how we can make a difference in this vast world. "What's the use? I can only take care of me." Exactly. In the healing of yourself, you affect all. Your higher frequency joins other frequencies resonating there, and soon those frequencies become the dominating frequencies.

Then change happens. A new leader is appointed that reflects and resonates with the mass vibration. New programming emerges representing the focus on health. Berlin walls come down. People get fed. New breakthroughs happen. We see bumper stickers focusing on "Peace is the answer" not "War is not the answer."

We no longer can allow our belief in separatism to undermine our responsibility. We are not here to save the world. We are here to heal ourselves. When each heals himself, we heal the whole. And the world is saved. Energy principles apply to the one and the One. And the one is the One.

Energy doesn't end at the borders of our bodies or our backyards. Energy is a whole, always seeking to be whole. Our fallacy is that we believe we must heal energy outside of ourselves to heal our world. In fact, it is the opposite. We can't save others. That is their choice alone. Each must choose his own experience. I AM.

That becomes confusing when we are called to help those less fortunate. Are we not called to serve? I think we must closely question our intention behind the service. Is it from unconditional love? Or are there hidden intentions to convert, dominate, judge, or economically advance through the guise of aid?

Again, we can only have dominion over ourselves, not anyone or anything else. We can only control our choices. We are in control when we are in trust and are able to go with the flow of Oneness energy, not when we're coming from fear that stops or diverts the energy of Oneness.

As in our individual lives, we want to take on responsibility that is not ours, which makes energy ineffective. True power of oneness becomes Force over the illusion of separate energy. We act out of the fear of being irresponsible, which focuses the energy away from creation of what we really want: wholeness. Individual becomes global. When I relinquish my ability to respond, I engage with the guys who flip me off on the freeway. I give up choice and get pissed off. When enough people get pissed off, we have riots. When enough people riot, we have mass internal unrest. Then we go to war to get "what we need" to be safe. It's all the same frequency shared by the individual and the mass consciousness. Mass consciousness made up of individual consciousness.

We are all pooling into the One Energy—the collective, the society, the world, and the universe. If we, and therefore our society, feel unworthy, add this to the vibrational match with all the rest of the people who are defining themselves as not being worthy, and soon we have a universe that is a big pool of energy that's not worthy of receiving what they want to manifest. Right now that looks like a world that believes we've got to have bombs, we're not safe, our stock market has to surpass your stock market, there's disease everywhere, and people are starving. Because the one pool grows so great, it starts to suck everybody into the pattern of not trusting, not being worthy, and not knowing we create our own lives. Until people start removing themselves on purpose and by choice from that definition of the One and start creating a higher perspective of the One by knowing they are their own creator, we don't create a new pool, a new world, or a new universe. As we recreate our own private world, our own personal world, we create the world with new perspectives, and we ultimately create a new world with higher perspectives and worthiness.

The highest definition that we can claim for ourselves and for the world is, "I AM Love. I AM the One Energy." When I put out the perception and the belief and the knowingness of my worthiness as the One, and you match that with your knowingness and your worthiness of the One, then we have created a world that knows its worth. Until that happens, we are still defining ourselves as separate and less than the One.

Let's take it back to my neighbor with the pool for a moment. Remember how we began engaging in a territorial disharmony around the parking issue? Basically, what happened was we were both saying to one another, "This is my property." "No, this is my property." (Not I AM a person who has enough to share.) Both of us went into a mini energetic battle. Essentially it wasn't anybody's property; it was just a piece of property. The energy around this was "I don't want to be peaceful with you because you have what I want. I only want peace if I can get what I want, which means I'm not worthy enough to love myself enough and the Universe enough to know that I can get what I want while you get what you want." In that moment, regardless of how my neighbor defined himself, was my opportunity to choose. Do I want peace, or reaction? Once I enter the reactionary phase, I have moved out of choice and balance. It then becomes about him, when it is only about me. My choice. My perspective. My love. My I AM.

When we move out of that moment of choice, which is the moment of creation, we shift into a perspective that will not, and does not, and is not manifesting the world that we want. False IMing. So neither of us is able to create and allow for peace, which is truly what we want to give ourselves because we're worthy of living in bliss.

For example, when my perspective changed to the realization and the recognition that there was more to this situation, I was able to choose a higher direction for my energy. I chose to choose that! When our perspective changes, we may not get, in the moment, what we think we want, but we do get what we want in the ultimate outcome: a higher vibration for ourselves, for the world, and, ultimately, everyone living in harmony and all sharing the parking space.

A lot of times the biggest wall in our way is that we just simply don't want to, refuse to, or will not move to change our perspective. (I AM choosing to stay stuck.) We all know that oftentimes in relationships our perspective is, "Wow, this is a great relationship. This is everything I need." Ten years into that relationship, everything's changed. Our perspective of what we need has changed because we've changed. We've grown. We've learned. Our consciousness has moved. Therefore, the perspective of what we want and what we need to demand around our worthiness shifts. If we can choose to move into different perspectives, every moment of every day of our lives, any time that we perceive that the world is not serving us, then we can open ourselves up to the perception that every moment is serving us when we choose the higher perspective and regain balance and choice.

Our perceptions are pooling themselves into the One Energy along with all other people. The world creates itself out of this pool of energy—its Collective Consciousness. Right now, much of the Collective Consciousness lives in the fears of unworthiness and the fears that we have to force and control and demonstrate our worthiness in the world. That pool has created itself as war, freeway shootings, and school shootings. All of these are just magnified manifestations of my neighbor and myself. These in turn pull us back into that pool of fear, which lowers our vibrations, which in turn create more fear and more territorial wars, which create more battles and more fears, which make us continually feel unworthy because we're in fear. Nobody is living in peace because we're not living in love. We're all living with limited perspectives, and the pool of our perspectives is perpetuated. I AM an unhappy world.

Unless we consciously know and choose to keep directing the Creative Force to deliver what we want, which is love, while choosing the vibration of love itself, love will elude us. As soon as the mass vibration of consciousness, masses of us, stands up in a new perspective and say, "I AM choosing to know that I am worthy. I AM choosing to attract everything in my universe to me that creates worthiness, creates love, creates me knowing that there's enough, and creates me knowing that there is no separation, only love, only the One," then we will

109

create ourselves as people who elect officials that reflect our perspectives. We will create ourselves in a universe that reflects what the mass majority is holding around those beliefs. Therefore, when we create newer perspectives from a place of worthiness we allow manifestation of everything we are claiming that we want now.

Fear of Power

So why are we reluctant to claim, "I AM Source?"

We haven't experienced our light and our power in a very long time. Most of us simply don't remember the truthfulness of our higher being. We don't know how to define ourselves. Many of us grew up with parents who were not enlightened: parents who also had been taught force instead of true creative power. Parents who lived in fear and lack.

These were our first and most authoritative teachers. Our "gods." We took them at their word that they were teaching us the truth. They couldn't. They hadn't been taught the truth. So we seek their approval by adhering to their "truths." Just when we get their approval, we grow up, and the next stage of life sets in and we must move on from making our parents happy and live our own lives.

We don't know—because we've never been taught—that we are in co-creation with Source. Everything has been filtered through our parents, so we keep looking outside of ourselves for that lost approval, instead of looking within ourselves. Parents never tell us they are there for short-term guidance. They can't. No one told them. When we break away from that relationship, we initially experience the power of who we really are and it scares the hell out of us.

That, I believe, is the biggest fear that's holding us in non-allowing. The fear of our power and that we will abuse that power. Our power to create and the responsibility inherent in that power. It's the knowing that we create everything in our lives in partnership with Source. We do this with a simple formula. I choose, I direct, I believe, and I allow. For example, I choose abundance. I direct clearly what I want in regards to money. I claim abundance in my life. I live in the vibration of abundance 24/7.

For some of us, that may mean $100 a week. For others, it's $1 million a month. We define what is highest for ourselves. It's what's right for us. It's like medicine. One pill doesn't serve everybody. We have to find out what our body chemistry and energetic system responds to. We have to be very clear about what we want. We have to say to the Creative Force, "This is what I want, create this for me now. I AM _____." Then we need to step back and allow the Creative Force to deliver instead of needing to be in control every step of the way. That's the old way. Our parents' way. Because we are all One Energy, we are directing ourselves as part of the Creative Force. We are Creation because it's all One Energy. Once the direction is given, you've got to know that it's done. Already. You release it and allow it to come in, any way it wants to come in. Your job is to receive what you know as already manifested energetically. Do we mail a letter more than once in fear of it not arriving? Keep placing our dinner order over and over at the restaurant? Keep trying to get pregnant when we're already due? No. Of course not! Yet most of us live 24/7 in "keep trying." Trying and doing are mutually exclusive. Let go and know.

My series was a wonderful stepping-stone. The Universe created it, with me, to get me back into the game, to build my self-esteem. As brilliant as it was, it didn't run a second year. For me, there were still perceptions of worthiness I needed to recreate. I am sure the cancellation of the show reflected other opportunities to grow for the rest of the cast also. I needed to celebrate my self-worth so all other energy could come forth to do the same.

That experience did serve in redirecting my path. I signed with newer, bigger agents. Movies opened up for me again. As

I write this, I am still celebrating the journey as I learn to celebrate my worthiness more each day. Sometimes the process is a real challenge.

It's sometimes confusing just how to merge these principals with the physical world. It's a fact we live in a world of "take action." Most of us claim what we want, direct it, and say, "Create this for me now." Then we go into the beliefs of, "I've got to do this and I've got to do that. Where is it? I'm going to make this happen if it's the last thing I do." Vibrationally, we drop out of "knowing" because we're trying to "get to." That throws us out of balance, which sends desperate IMs. We're not allowing what we want to come to us in the way the universe can creatively bring it to us, in the highest form and best timing.

Sometimes the Universe is co-creating with us for our highest good by not manifesting for us. When that happens, we energetically get redirected and have to regroup. Oftentimes, I have been despondent over a job loss I thought would have been "it." Usually I hear what a nightmare the set was or that the project didn't end up going. I was being protected from a vibrational waste of energy. Sometimes, great projects have eluded me that are, well, great projects. The Universe doesn't give us what isn't ours no matter how much we push. When we remain in the trust of "it's all good," we co-create something else.

When we take action, we must vigilantly do it from a balanced, clearly directed intention. In other words, I attend auditions, send out pictures, and network while I am in the belief that the work and career is already manifested. I hold the perspective that, as I am taking physical action, the perfection of manifestation is being created in the moment. This consistent, clear direction while holding myself in high, playful vibration is creation. As I am holding the direction and vibration and doing the physical requirements, I get a matching manifestation. You can't just dress the part. You have to believe the part. I AM.

Can you feel the difference between, "Okay, I'm going to do what I need to do and I'm going to let it go," and, "Okay, I'm going to go make it happen, damn it?" It's a whole different vibrational place to live. Be careful that the physical requirements don't lower your vibrations and throw you out of balance. Behind working hard is the fear of not getting unless I do. We must work smarter in the ease and expectation of good that allows creation. This allowingness is something that we've never been taught. On the contrary, we've been taught that we've got to struggle. We've got to do it because if we don't do it, nobody's going to do it for us. Our actions get fueled by desperation and fear. Wrong IM.

Control

Control: the power to direct or determine; to hold in check; to test or verify.

When we apply the above definitions toward one's self, we move into creation. When we apply them outside of ourselves, we move into the illusion of control. Obviously, if the only energy we have dominion over is our own, when we go to control others, we simply meet with resistance.

When we exercise direction over our own energy, hold ourselves in check regarding our intentions and reactions, and use the outside influences only as a test to verify our own energies and guide our co-creation, then we move into the only control available to us. The highest form of control, as it's defined, is the I AM. We are always in control when we're in the flow of energy: all is good, all is guiding us, and death is merely a transition. When we experience everything from a place of trust, by its very definition then, we are in control. We are choosing to direct our lives. I AM. And trusting manifestation.

When I used to go to an audition, I thought I had to be in control of the room. I know I have to be in trust of myself and

the material. I have to fully be in trust with myself and LET
GO. Let the material flow through me. Let the character flow
out of me. It's all about flow and trust.

Whenever I try to control the creativity too much, I don't
book the job. When you unequivocally trust the energy so you
can remain in, and with, the flow, you stay in the place of
knowingness. It really forces you to "know," because it forces
you to be one with yourself and all energy. You cannot
separate yourself into watching or judging or manipulating any
of the energy—including self—in any way. You are simply
part of the One, unfolding in each moment. Your limiting
mental perspectives disappear into true beingness.

Whether I get the part or not, I am in control of my life
through the knowing that it is all good. When we act from that
place of unconditional trust, we don't move into the fear that
cripples us. We are in trust that we are always taken care of.

If we fear that we're going to die or not be taken care of,
we are directing the I AM energy, through that fear, to create a
world where we live in fear and are not taken care of. Through
our perspective that we are not taken care of, we create chaos
and a world of false control, called force. You can see the
power of this belief when it comes to the Collective
Consciousness. Together, the fear becomes
a collective pool which creates our world.

The principles that serve the individual serve the whole.
Let's say there are twenty people in a room, and four of them
are holding the perceptions that they will be hurt by the others.
They live in that expectation. That fear. Let's suppose that four
others know they are always protected and taken care of. They
live in peacefulness of trust, that there is something being
served here.

Right at this moment, we have four in fear and four in
peace. There is a balance within the room of opposing
vibrations. It is obvious to see that the energies of the twelve
other people begin to be extremely important in defining the
frequency of the room as a whole. If eight more people begin

vibrating in fear and mistreatment, the frequencies in the room as a whole become unbalanced toward fear. That is why the perspectives, directions, and choices of each are so vital to the whole. No one has control over another except through his own choice.

Force is where we move into false "control" out of fear.

Force	**Power**
Do this because I say so.	I stay in balance as the example of creation.
You have to be responsible or get out.	I allow you to choose for yourself as I focus on being balanced within.
We have to go to war to maintain peace.	We vibrate in peace, focus in peace and create peace through our energy (e.g. Gandhi.)
I have to keep control to be safe.	I am always in control and safe as I trust in the Universe.
I have to make them.	I have to heal me.
I have to save the world.	I have to heal me.
I have to show them they're wrong.	I have to heal me.

When we move into true co-creation with the flow of the One Energy first, then we attract to us the divine right people to support us on our path. It is imperative that you serve yourself as your own god that you are, the self-healer that you are. "To thine own self be true." Look within. That is where all the work is done. I AM Source.

Chapter 10

The Creation Equation

"I honor the healing powers of self and others…Until I found the phenomena that started to explain these healings, I, too, called them miracles. And then I learned from using my own loving, healing energies that the miracle lay within."
Valerie Hunt, *Infinite Mind*, p275

"All these things I do, and even greater things than these shall you do, if you believe in I AM"
John 14:12

"We even construct space and time."
David Bohm's conclusion,
Holographic Universe, p55.

WE HAVE ESTABLISHED THAT SCIENCE and spirituality are sharing similar understandings regarding co-creation. All the principles of positive thinking, prayer, visualization, and the importance of focus and attention have been assessed as dynamic elements in the creation of energy.

It is my firm belief that the missing key here is conscious direction of the I AM as Divine Love. I AM Divine Love.

In this chapter, we will offer a template to assist you in the journey and navigation of any goal, any creation.

Let's review quickly what we know:

- Everything is energy.
- We can alter or transmute energy.
- We do this consciously by directing the energy to manifest what we want.
- We choose to live in forgiveness and gratitude.
- The frequencies that we vibrate in, sometimes called emotions, frame of mind, outlook, or love of life, must match and complement our intention. For example, saying we want to have perfect health and being angry or despondent does not "match up." Creation becomes limited or thwarted.
- We must consciously choose to remain focused on only what we want until manifestation occurs.
- We choose to believe and know.
- We choose to love ourselves and to be LOVE.

These few things are the ingredients for our creation. If there is any resistance to these truths, we need to balance ourselves before continuing. We do that by looking at the listed points, and knowing the following:

1. Our intention is to create the life we want while holding the higher intention of love for the good of all.
2. We are choosing to heal totally.
3. We are choosing to release all resistance and move into flow.
4. We are directing the Creative Force/God/Source to create these desires for the highest good of all. I AM Divine Love.

Now that all resistance has been balanced, and our clear intention to heal and love has been claimed, let us move to the template for all creation. Basically, we simply must direct or claim the I AM around our desire. I AM IMing what I want.

I'm going to walk you through some sessions so you have a deeper understanding of how this process works and what, exactly, happens when you claim the I AM.

Bill

I asked Bill what he wanted to work on. "Success. It seems like I get so far and then nothing pans out." I asked Bill what he wanted. "I want to be successful." I asked him what that meant. "Well, you know, that I finally achieve what I try to. That I get to where I want to go." That was the best he could do, so I moved on. What's in your way? "I don't know," he lamented, "I work so hard but nothing happens. I make little strides but not the big success I want. I want to be successful more than anything."

So, let's break down Bill's statements:
1. He wants to be successful more than anything.
2. He works "so hard."
3. He gets "so far."
4. Nothing pans out.
5. He makes little strides but not big ones.

These are all beliefs and fears being held somewhere in Bill's energetic field. They are limiting Bill's creation.

Through kinesiology, Bill and I were directed to go to the age of four. Something happened with Bill's mother that was the beginning of these limitations. After a series of questions, Bill's mouth fell open. "Oh my God," he exclaimed. "My birthday fell late in the year, and I could have started school at four. I really, really wanted to go to school. I remember my mom saying to me that I just wasn't responsible enough to go to school. I didn't make my bed or keep my room clean or help with the dishes. When I could take care of myself, I could 'move ahead!'"

Those were his mother's words. She was defining him as a person who was "not responsible enough to move ahead." And Bill had been defining himself that way ever since.

Could Bill have balanced everything regarding "being a success" without this information? Yes. By directing the Creative Force, we direct it to find all frequencies, in all

119

energy, in all dimensions, for all time. Source finds the blocks, heals the frequencies, and allows energy to flow without resistance toward creation of our direction. Simply holding the intention and direction heals the blocks. When Bill looked at his limiting beliefs, directed the energy to balance, and claimed "I AM" the positives around his desires, all beliefs balanced, and his vibrations tested positive. He could now focus on what he wanted without resistance.

Now Bill focuses on,

- I AM Successful.
- Success is easy and effortless. (So he doesn't have to "work so hard.")
- Everything pans out.
- I go all the way.
- I make big strides.

Again, we have taken his limiting beliefs, raised the vibrations creating those blocks, restated all in the positive, and directed him to be happy, as he claims what he wants until it appears. Remember, it is a process. And it gets simpler.

Feeling

Jeremy

Jeremy sat there. He had this kind of energetic attitude of defensiveness. "I don't know," he replied. "I don't know what I want to work on." Then he broke into tears. "I just don't want to feel this way anymore. I hate feeling this way."

I asked him to describe the "feeling."

- Hopeless
- Despondent
- Angry
- "Like crying"

And he didn't know why. I told him to focus on the feeling and what the opposite positive would "feel" like.

- Lots of energy
- Playing golf
- The beach
- Great sex

I smiled. We claimed the I AM. He looked at me. He smiled. Then he broke out into tears of joy. He said he felt "lighter."

It is possible to direct the energy whether you know exactly where to direct it or not. Hold the feeling. You know you don't want that feeling. You want to feel joy and love and empowerment! Direct the energy to create that. Claim I AM joy and love and empowerment. Keep focused on only that! Be love.

My Example

I wanted to focus on perfect health. Here are my limiting beliefs extracted from my self-talk.
- Physical healing would be a miracle and who am I to do that?
- Everyone in my family suffers from backaches and high blood pressure.
- I really can't believe the entire world can heal themselves physically. (If I can, then everyone can. So I'm in conflict with myself.)
- I don't know who I am without these health issues. I've had them so long. They are how I "define" myself now.

Now rewrite these statements into the positive, as I've done below.

- I AM worthy to create physical healing.
- I define my own perfect health (as a separate entity from my family.)
- I claim that I (and the world) heals physically.
- I AM defining myself as perfect health.
- I keep focused and claiming until it manifests in my life.
- If I begin moving into doubt or fear, I simply claim, "I AM Divine Love."
- I live in love. I AM love.

I direct the Energy to deliver this to me now. I claim: "I AM Divine Love." I raise my "happy" vibration so the Universe wants to play. I remain focused on what I want.

Writing this for the book was an enlightening experience. Even teaching the work every day, I still am awed by the process of discovery about our hidden energy. For the first time I realized there was a kind of "bonding" going on with my family. Everyone in the family had high blood pressure and back problems. I was defining myself as part of the family because I shared in these maladies! My conscious mind couldn't believe that I still doubted my self-worth in physical healing and miraculous accomplishments. I feel I've had so many. Yet the physical aspect of life seems to be the greatest challenge of trust. I know I must believe (as we all do) that the world is healing itself now, or that manifestation is thwarted in some way. I know we must look away from the facade of world hunger and focus on world nourishment. Yet, I still wrote down this thought! It is a reminder of the continuing process in our enlightenment journey.

This is very exciting for me because it reveals yet another layer I can redirect and heal. That leads to more joyous creation of manifestation for myself and the world. Moving out of my own way excites me!

Please take time to write yours now. Remember, the golden insights will come more instinctively rather than intellectually. Just write. There is no one to judge. There is only you who has already claimed, "I want to heal."

We are asking ourselves to literally redefine the very basis of how we have thought the world to be created: from the outside to the inside. We are choosing to know it is the opposite: our world is created from within and extends outward.

We simply need to be conscious of our own limiting energy, our beliefs, feelings, and judgments, choose to recreate them, and redirect the energy to the positive creation.

The more we practice this, the more it becomes a habit. Like anything, it can be a challenge at first to be conscious every waking moment, but as we see our lives changing for the better and we become happier, we want to live in the space of constant co-creation. We want to stay in the higher vibration.

Start practicing in little ways. Make it a game. Start catching yourself every time you have a negative thought about yourself or your life, or when you notice that you are not manifesting your desires. Begin using the I AM to IM Source to recreate your energy as positive, and begin "playing" with what you want.

Next, try being conscious of all those annoying little judgments of other people throughout the day: the grocery clerk, the guy who cuts in front of you to get the parking space, the teenager in your life with attitude. Remember! Your intention is to heal you. You are raising your vibration out of judgment toward others so they will not be attracted into your energy field. It helps in getting parking spaces!

It used to drive my daughter nuts. She and her friends would be with me, and I'd say out loud, "OK, God, find me a parking space right now." I'd hear hushed whispers about what a weird mom I was emerging from the backseat. Then my daughter would say, "I know. She's weird. But it works," as we were pulling into a space.

Make it a game with yourself. How many points can you rack up at the end of a day by realizing a negative belief, feeling, judgment, or expectation and redirecting it to the positive? How can you love yourself more? The difference in your energy will be amazing, and the response of all other energy, from the people and pets to finances and health, will start to turn around dramatically. Because other positive energy will want to "play" with yours!

The Answer

Now I want to share with you the secret behind all manifestation. If prayer, visualization, visioning, and affirmations aren't working, this is the reason why. It is the secret that makes *The Secret* work. It is the bleep in *What the Bleep Do We Know*. It is the answer. We have always had it. We have always known it, but unless we are it, nothing else works.

Love yourself.

I know. It really is that simple.

We Are Taught to Limit Self Love

When we are born, most of us are lucky enough to be truly loved and celebrated. We are doted upon. We are the center of our Universe. It is truly, all about us.

That lasts just as long as society deems it acceptable, and then the training of limitation begins. At around two, we begin the indoctrination of "how to give up the self." We are taught not to interrupt and not to speak up for what we want. If we are "good" we give the toy we want to the other kid, and we're "bad" if we love ourselves enough to keep it and make ourselves happy. We wear clothes that aren't comfortable or clothes that embarrass us. We conform to what others believe is right for us. We are taught these things "define" us, instead of trusting our authentic selves to be enough.

We are pushed into school before we are ready and urged to study hard so we'll be good enough to make it. Message: we aren't good enough being who we are. What we do makes us good enough.

Then we enter the adult world, which further defines us by how much we make, not WHO WE ARE.

The constant failures and successes and achievements and disappointments make us forget that we are God. We are Source. We are the Creative Force. And therefore, we are Divine Love.

If all energy is one, Divine Love IS Self Love. We were created to love ourselves and experience the magnificence of love for everything: each other, the oceans, the animals, the trees and all of creation. We experience other love through self-love. Yes, indeed, to thine own self be true. What we learned as our first definition is the highest truth.

God is love.

And we are it. Until we can throw our arms around ourselves in adoration, how can we truly create what we want for ourselves?

The Polarity of I Love Me/I Don't

You know how ridiculous it is to think we can manifest without self-love? Let's review some of our day to day thoughts:

I'm too fat.

I'm too old.

I don't have enough money.

I don't have a relationship. I must not be worth it.

I don't have a well body.

I don't have a young body.

I should have been a success by now.

I don't have the house I want.

Etc.

Etc.

Etc.

THEN we have the audacity to say to Creation: give me what I want.

Try it. Look in the mirror and state all the limitations and fears and negative beliefs you have. List all the people you are angry with and choose not to forgive. List all the people and things that are "holding you back."

Then look at yourself—knowing you are God—and have the audacity to say, "Give me everything I want now, please. Because I deserve it." I bet you can't do it without smiling. You truly experience how silly it is.

When we have accepted the limitations and judgments of the world, we choose to define ourselves as a part of God that does not love itself. That does not honor itself. Or celebrate itself. Or manifest for itself because it is gloriously worthy.

It is now up to our individual choice to stand up and proclaim: I love myself!

When I was looking for a pre-school for my daughter, I visited over thirty. I knew I would know when I saw the "right" one. The next to the last school I checked out was called Magic Years. These are, I thought, magic years. What a great name.

The day I audited, the teacher was leading them in a song that went like this:

I love myself,

The way I AM.

There's nothing for me to change,

I'll always be

The perfect me.

There's nothing to rearrange.

I'm beautiful and capable

Of being the best me I can,

And I love myself,
Just the way I AM.

The teacher dismissed them for recess and on his way out, one of the little boys ran straight into me. Looking up, without missing a beat, he proclaimed with arms stretched wide, "Hi Lady, I love me," and ran out to play.

Needless to say, my daughter ended up at that school. But notice who remembers the song!

It was a message I knew, but had forgotten. It is a message we all know, and must remember.

Love yourself.

All else will follow. Self-Love is love of the Divine. It is Creation itself. With that beginning element, all else is created.

Creation Equation

The simplest Creation Equation for everything is:
1. Love yourself.
2. Feel happy.
3. Be clear about what you want.
4. Be conscious to balance fears, and limitations.
5. Direct yourself/Creative Force to create your desires (or something better!) with love for all.
6. Allow yourself to receive anything and everything without expectation or limitation to "how it should look." Remember: you love yourself so much, you're worth it.

You direct all the above with the statement:
I AM Divine Love

Too easy? Too nebulous? Then I put the question to you: would it be all right if your life got easier? Would it be all right if your life got happier? It is up to you to choose.

Like ET, once we choose to get back home, and consciously send the direction out, we manifest our desires. We get back home. To our love, to peace, to knowing we are Creation.

Some of us will start seeing manifestation in some things instantly. For others of us, it will take a bit longer. It simply depends on our resistance. Keep focused on what you want and keep disciplined in this practice of the Creation Equation. You will see results simply in the way you view the world. Your life will be more joyful. You will be creating your life as Co-Creator of your life with Source.

Epilogue

Individual Creation and the World

IF WE ARE SOURCE AND everyone else is Source, then we are all Source defining itself in different ways.

In the past, when those different definitions agreed with each other, we have called it Source. When they have disagreed, we have called it "them." Since all is One Energy, the disagreement and agreement are One Energy: Source. So if we are in disagreement, we are defining ourselves as people who want to be separate from ourselves. And Source. This is a rather accurate definition of our world.

When events happen in our world—natural catastrophes, financial decay, terrorism, and health epidemics, our definitions are often altered. People are brought together through necessity and changing perception. The people we have defined as "them" become "us," as in all societies before and after world wars. For example, the Japanese enemy of Pearl Harbor is now our economic partner in multitudes of venues with the United States.

After 9/11 and the terrorist attacks throughout the world, countries not working together began defining themselves as "partners" in the war on terrorism. As AIDS crossed racial, economic and sexual barriers, it became a worldwide project to wipe out the disease that had so easily allowed people to call it just a "homosexual disease."

As these individual definitions change, the frequencies being directed into the One Energy are mutating also. The vibrations are changing from "them" to "us." The pointed finger of blame and victim consciousness morph into open arms of compassion and acceptance. Of course, the opposite also occurs. The good become the bad, the ally the enemy. The yin and yang of the all too familiar human pattern keeps rotating and changing.

The challenge for us here is to realize that we are the forces defining ourselves individually, which, in turn, define the state of our countries and therefore the world.

But we refuse to accept that responsibility.

We want it to be the world's fault. We believe it is the world that creates the circumstances that force our countries to be the way they are. That sets up our societies in which we must define ourselves in certain ways to exist. Translation: we are victims of something "outside" of us. We are "outside" of our creation. This separation of self and creation perpetuates the situation and clouds the options. Even for world peace.

Let's take for a moment, the issue of world hunger. Suppose every person in the world defined themselves as a person who knows how to feed everyone, as someone who knows there is enough food to feed the world. Let's say we all know this. Therefore, the Collective Consciousness knows this. Therefore, the frequency with which the world is vibrating is everyone can be fed. If that vibration is dominant in the world, people will get fed.

There is enough food. Everyone knows the food is being grown and is available, but politics get in the way of distribution. Economics get in the way of distribution. False control gets in the way of distribution. We accept all these reasons that people are not getting fed and we stop creating what we know is possible!

You ask, "How can I make a difference?" We make a difference because it is our vibration that is added to the whole vibration of Source. When enough of us add that knowing to the whole, the whole then knows. What the Whole knows is either the problem or the solution. We decide!

Until we all choose to know—before the manifestation—the manifestation doesn't have the power of vibration to appear.

I know + the majority knows = Source knows.

Source is waiting for us to choose what we know so it can manifest itself as the majority vibration. The urgency for us all to define our knowingness is apparent. We are literally creating our world.

Knowingness

Knowing isn't intellectual. It doesn't sit and "figure out" how to. It just does. It knows.

A baby "knows" to cry when it needs something. A dog "knows" to lick a wound. The flowers "know" when to bloom. Somewhere, we "know" we are creators and in a constant creative interplay with the Universe.

I define me→ the Universe responds→ I react to the way the Universe responds→ I redefine me→ the Universe responds.

We can't try to know. We just know. We can't get there from our heads, only from our heart vibration.

We have all had moments of knowing in our lives. I knew I would have my daughter even though six "experts" said I wouldn't. When my friend was diagnosed with cancer, she never faltered in her knowing that she would be fine. And she was. She created her health instead of being in reaction to her disease.

Our places of knowing are peaceful and undeniable. Take a moment to get quiet and direct your subconscious to reacquaint you with your knowing. It will feel calm, powerful, all-knowing—like it "just is." Dwell here for a moment. This is a place where you know you are creating, where indeed you are Creation. A beautiful sunset, a moment with a favorite animal, a kiss—we all have moments of blissful beingness that transcend being.

The love vibration is the highest vibration of creation possible. To live in love is to live in the knowing of creation every moment. It is Creation. It is the knowing that no matter what we experience as reality, we are creating reality at that same moment. When we live in the moment of creation, reality becomes redefined. It's all here to serve.

I see the world hungry.

I know in this moment I create the world being fed with my vibration.

I therefore see the world being fed unconditionally.

I see the world fed.

My vibrations affect others.

They begin seeing the world fed.

Their vibrations affect others.

They begin seeing the world fed.

The hundredth monkey phenomenon occurs.

The majority sees the world fed.

The world is fed.

Obviously, the same principle applies to world peace, health, and abundance. What we focus on and the vibrations we live in create the world. Not the other way around.

Some interesting points to ponder from this perspective:

Are we focused on the end of the world or are we focused on creating a brave, new world?

Are we living in fear of former predictions or are we creating a new definition of life?

Are we becoming withdrawn into self-protection or are we realizing we are in creation together?

Are we focused on fear or love?

Are we victor or victim?

It is our duty—our right—to responsibly take the creation of this world into re-creation of the world we visualize and desire. We must define ourselves as the Source that is the creation in the highest love possible for all. (Highest intention: create the life you want while holding the higher intention of love for the good of all.)

Source is asking us to make the choice that only we can make. The choice to live. In peace. In love. In co-creation. We are the Source we have been praying to.
I claim:
I AM Creation.
I AM love.
I AM peace.
I AM that I AM.
I love myself enough to create the world I choose.
And so it is.

Glossary

Allowing – Letting the world work for you: getting out of your own way by releasing judgments and limited thinking; Receiving all life as "yes"

Beingness – The art of being Collective Consciousness – the energy of the One that is defined by the collective energy of the all: the energy of the mass that creates from shared beliefs/fears/expectations

Conscious Creation – Being conscious of your thoughts, beliefs and fears so you are always at choice in choosing WHAT you create, making the creation "conscious."

Creation – Energy is always in the state of creation. Therefore, we are always creating whether we know it or not.

Creative Force – the energy that creates: also referred to as God, Spirit, Higher Consciousness, Buddha, Source, Atman, Universal Truth, etc.

Electron – an extremely small, negatively charged particle supposed to be or to contain the unit of negative electricity

Energy – All that is: everything is energy. Energy can be transformed through specific direction, i.e. water to ice to steam. Thoughts are energy that is also changed by specific choice and direction.

Enlightenment – An unlimited mind, new thoughts, full realization of all possibilities: oneness with all energy; Knowing you are the creative force

Focus – where your attention is consciously or unconsciously

Frequency – It carries out your vibration into the atmosphere. Like a radio frequency, the clearer you "send out" your vibration, the more accurately the Universe receives the message.

Higher Self – The part of you that knows, that is remembering you are the Creative Force in embodiment: it is not limited by the mind, and accessed by the heart

I~M System - The system whereby we communicate with the Universe through our feelings, verbal expressions, thought processes or the vibrations we send out regardless of whether the action is conscious or unconscious. Example: Every time we communicate, "I AM_____ " we are sending an instant message (IM) to the Universe directing it to create what we just stated.

IM, IMing, - acronyms for Instant Message and Instant Messaging

Instant Message (IM) - Conscious or unconscious communication with the Universe directing it to create in our lives whatever follows the words, "I AM _____."

Kinesiology - the art of connecting to the Higher Energy to get clear, concise answers removed from the lower plane consciousness of ego. It is done through testing the strength and resistance of muscles. If a statement is truthful energetically, it strengthens you and also your muscles. If it is not, it weakens you. Organs, food, thoughts and beliefs, which are all energy, can be tested with this method. It is a powerful way to discern subconscious energy that may be weakening you.

Lightworker – the name encompasses all kinds of various healers that are working as and with the Creative Force for the balance of energy

Limiting Beliefs – Beliefs we have that limit our perspectives, which limit our possibilities. For example: money is bad or you get sick as you get older

New Age – referring to the new ideas, new thoughts, and new understandings of our role in creation; departure from traditional religious beliefs

Particle – Referring to subatomic particles, or any various units below the size of an atom

Pendulum – usually a gemstone of some kind suspended by a chain or string. The chain is held between the thumb, index finger, and middle finger while the stone dangles. Actually, you can even use a necklace or a tea bag. Each person has a distinct swing pattern for "yes," which mirrors the strength of the arm in kinesiology, and a "no," which represents weak muscles. Therefore, by using yes/no statements, this allows a person to test energy on their own.

Perspective – How you look at life: the emotions and reality you choose to see in any situation Is the glass half full or half empty? Is your life joyful or painful? All is dictated by your perspective, which is a choice.

Polarities – The perspective that there are opposites in energy; In reality, polarities do not exist on the Higher Dimensions of understanding. There is One Energy which includes all. The need for right/wrong and good/evil creates separation and judgment

Proton – a subatomic particle bearing a unitary, or electronic, positive charge of electricity

137

Source – Another term for Creative Force, it is the energy all creation flows from.

Thought – The brain's stream of consciousness: it can be conscious or unconscious. Thought is where creation begins.

Vibrations/Vibrational – the movement of energy that telegraphs messages and directions to the Creative Force. When we "vibrate" anger, we send messages to the Creative Force to create anger. When we "vibrate" love, we send messages to create love. Emotions/feelings are indicators of our vibratory state.

Dee Wallace

Originally from Kansas City, Kansas, Dee Wallace is a proud graduate from the University of Kansas where she received her B.A. in Education and Theatre. As an actress, her thirty years of movie magic have touched countless lives.

Having more than 100 television and film credits to her name, Dee has collaborated with some of the most brilliant minds in the industry, including Steven Spielberg, Peter Jackson, Wes Craven, and Stephen King. Her many film credits include such classics as 10, The Hills Have Eyes, The Howling, Cujo, The Frighteners, and most notably her starring role in one of America's most celebrated films, E.T. The Extra-Terrestrial.

Dee is a talented actress, clairaudient healer, and a much sought after motivational speaker who currently hosts the incredibly popular "Conscious Creation Radio"• on 7th Wave Network, "Bright Light" on the Awakening Zone Network as well as her own monthly segment on the internationally acclaimed Healing With the Masters.
For more information, please visit www.iamdeewallace.com

Other Books Published
by
Ozark Mountain Publishing, Inc.

Continue for more books by Ozark Mountain Publishing, Inc.

For more information about any of the above titles, soon to be released titles, or
other items in our catalog, write or visit our website:

OZARK
MOUNTAIN
PUBLISHING

PO Box 754
Huntsville, AR 72740
www.ozarkmt.com
1-800-935-0045/479-738-2348
Wholesale Inquiries Welcome